ALL CHEESES GREAT AND SMALL

ALEX JAMES

ALL CHEESES GREAT AND SMALL

A LIFE LESS BLURRY

FOURTH ESTATE • *London*

First published in Great Britain by
Fourth Estate
An imprint of HarperCollins*Publishers*
77–85 Fulham Palace Road
London W6 8JB
www.4thestate.co.uk

1 3 5 7 9 10 8 6 4 2

A catalogue record for this book is
available from the British Library

ISBN 978-0-00-745312-2

Typeset in Sabon with Populaire display by
G&M Designs Limited, Raunds, Northamptonshire
Printed in Great Britain by
Clays Ltd, St Ives plc

Find out more about HarperCollins and the environment at
www.harpercollins.co.uk/green

FOR CLAIRE NEATE JAMES

CONTENTS

AUTUMN

WINTER

SPRING

SUMMER

AUTUMN

CHAPTER 1

HOUSE WITH A HUNDRED ROOMS

The end of the week, the end of summer: it was warm. Traffic crawling and brawling round the outside of Oxford. I stopped for fuel: the stench of petrol and the glare from the concrete apron.

I'd watched the white van stagger to a halt as the driver slammed the brakes on. I'd watched as it began to reverse towards me. There was the moment I knew he was going to hit me, and then I was flying backwards as the van smashed through the front of the old BMW I was sitting in. I'd been reversed into at high speed. Strange. There was another dent to add to the collection on the back of the van and the front of the BMW had completely caved in. Steam was hissing out of the radiator.

I wasn't hurt, but I was furious that I might have been, and even more furious about the car. I leapt out onto the concrete and began to call the driver names. Many names. There were two of them in the van. They both got out.

'Prove it,' said one.

'You just drove into us,' said the other.

It was hot and the roads were packed. I had the keys to my new life in my pocket. I bought half a dozen bottles of water from the cashier and stopped every five miles, every three, every one – as often as was necessary to top up the radiator while the temperature gauge hovered around the red. Crawling up the sides of apparently endless valleys. One more hill, one more dale until by fits and spurts I must have been pretty much at the middle of England: the very middle. Here, you might easily think that what is really quite a small island continues forever and ever. I coasted the last mile down the side of the last valley towards my new home. There were gypsies camping on the roadside at the top of the drive oblivious to the car doing ten miles an hour with steam coming out of the radiator. An old lady was doing some washing and was bent over with her back-side hanging out of her full skirt.

I knew the car was a write-off. I just needed it to get me home, or what I was about to call home. Because I'd just got married and swapped a London townhouse, with no garden, for a rambling farm. Why would I do that? It seemed straightforward when we were signing the paper-work. I thought that everyone wanted to move to the coun-try and live in a cottage with the roses around the door.

What I was doing was blindingly obvious to me, but when I'd started to try and explain it to other people it seemed no one else thought so. I had to answer lots of questions. My friends looked at me long and hard, like I'd started speaking a foreign language.

It wasn't until about the seventh time that Blur went to Japan that I managed to get out to the countryside there. 'I'd like to go out into the country,' I'd say hopefully, every time I arrived in Tokyo as soon as my hangover kicked in. It seemed to me a perfectly simple wish but it didn't make any sense to my hosts. 'Where in the countryside exactly?' they would say, diligently, 'what you want to do?' I wanted to go to the middle of nowhere and do absolutely nothing. It was no more complicated than that. And that was what I was doing now, just on a larger scale.

I had always been a man of leisure. I grew up in Bournemouth, a tourist resort, and was at my happiest fiddling about in the New Forest, on beaches, on the sea, in coves and quarries where there was nothing remotely particular to do: just magnificent scenery, a fantastic stage with fantastic lighting. The backdrop of the sea and the open sky that soaks that world right through is an open invitation to relax and play. But it was as if – to the Japanese, a conscientious hardworking people – the idea of just venturing off towards nowhere, going somewhere that is beyond the bump and grind, beyond industry, beyond the workaday, just didn't really add up. At least, it took some explaining. 'Well, I don't really want to do anything: maybe walk around a bit, jump off some cliffs, throw some stones. You know, that kind of thing.' They'd looked at me strangely then, and they looked at me strangely now.

Around Blur's fifth Japanese tour I eventually got as far as a little spa town in the mountains, and it was well worth waiting for. Doing things in cities can be hit and miss, but going anywhere in the country is always a safe bet because there is nothing in nature that is not fantastically beautiful. You know what you're going to get. Even those parts of Iceland that smell a bit eggy are worth having a look at.

Home, since I'd left college, had been Covent Garden. A one-bedroom flat when I was poor, and a house in the next street when the band sold some records. Claire and I fell in love one weekend in the Cotswolds and got married nine months after we met. We bought the farm on our honeymoon, at which point Blur promptly disintegrated. So I arrived in the country with a woman I didn't really know. Well, kind of with her. She was at work. I, on the other hand, didn't currently have a job. My friends were disgusted that I'd stopped drinking for a bit to get married, and now I'd appalled them further by walking out on them altogether. People said things like: 'How can you be a farmer? You don't know anything about farms?' or 'How can you be a husband? You're an arsehole.'

The main reason for going to the country was to be with her. I didn't know anybody in the Cotswolds; I didn't really know anything. Living the quiet life would have driven me utterly mad until I met her. It wasn't until I wanted to get married that the countryside started to attract me for reasons other than as a hangover cure. I'd spent my entire adult life living in the West End: the most metropolitan part of the largest city in Europe. But I was only there when I wasn't tearing around other large cities on tour with the band and gradually I'd found that I'd become addicted to big cities, their glamour, drama and possibilities. Now, though, I was definitely ready for a change.

We'd looked at lots of places. When we first saw the farm, there were a lot of fish in tanks in the cellar. In fact it looked like the people might be moving because they needed somewhere with a bigger cellar. The place was chock-a-block with tanks at all angles, and pumps and manifolds gurgling away. The fish were the first thing we were shown when we came to view the place.

'Are there woods? Where are the woods?' said Claire. 'Ah, yes, the woods. I think we'll just start by having a quick look in the cellar, though,' said the vendor. The fish weren't included in the sale. He just wanted us to see them. He took the fish with him, or they took him. He really didn't want to sell the place, the farmer. Poor man had been a beef specialist: punched on the nose by BSE, then kicked in the face by foot and mouth. He'd spent the last ten years watching everything he'd spent his life building, slip through his fingers as his profits dwindled and his assets corroded. It had been the worst time in history to be a farmer. The place was a ruin, but he'd loved it and poured his life into it. He was crying as he handed over the key, that was in my pocket now.

I cut the dying engine as I pulled off the road and was suddenly aware I was arriving at a point of silence. Silence and stillness. The gentle sounds, the pulses and tunes that had been there all along revealed themselves to my conscious mind. Rabbits scattered as I coasted slowly and gently down the drive in the filthy, dying car, with the front caved in and the rear driver's side window missing from an earlier incident.

It was rural, properly rural. People had asked me where it was we were going and there was no easy way to describe it. There were no towns nearby – the Industrial Revolution skipped the Cotswolds. It was an area that had never been built up. I didn't really know where the Cotswolds began or ended, although Oxford was possibly involved and Cheltenham. It was pure English countryside and that means old money and dynastic families wherever you go, but it also had more than its fair share of billionaire trades-men, and lately, television personalities, film directors and media moguls.

I remember the feeling I had when I first walked into my first rented flat in Covent Garden. A thrilling sense that this must be mine and no particular inclination to leave when I'd finished looking around.

We'd looked at all kinds of houses from manors and mansions to cottages and space age barn conversions – we'd got used to looking for ways to escape before we'd even been shown the best spare. When you get the feeling of not wanting to leave, you've found a home. And it doesn't happen very much. Like meeting people you could fall in love with, or seeing chances to change your life. They're bound to come along but never very often, and when they do come you've got to spot them and go after them with everything you've got, even if it makes you feel and look ridiculous – which is also pretty much guaranteed.

I liked that old farmer. He had a particular quality of serenity, as cool and powerful as the morning sun, and we were all instantly at ease in this cobble of buildings all clustered around an ancient well, fields stretching in all directions through pasture and woodland, bordered to the east by the road and the west by a river. It was the first house we'd seen that was obviously a reluctant sale. We'd walked around the place with him. He never said anything was wonderful or great or useful, like all of the other people had, but it all was. We'd sat in bright gold sunshine in the ramshackle kitchen having a cup of tea. It was just nice, merely nice but I knew I was having the feeling. The feeling of wanting to stay somewhere. And as I rolled up the drive I was having the feeling again. I wanted to stay. It was enough to make my heart beat faster in the silence. I didn't even care about the car. I was where I wanted to be. I didn't know my way around the place. I knew I wanted it the moment I arrived. I'd been back three times and still only scratched the surface. There were a lot of rooms, a lot of buildings, most of which I still hadn't even set foot in.

It was a mad jumble of endless compartments and spaces. If you included every building there must have been way more than a hundred rooms. Not one of them was very grand, and only the kitchen, the bathroom and one of the bedrooms in the farmhouse itself had recently been in use. There were so many outbuildings, a bewildering amount, it was more like a village than a house, really. Many stone and slate stables falling into disrepair. Endless empty structures snaking around overgrown courtyards. Everything from a cathedral-sized stone barn that looked as permanent as a mountain, to something that had been made out of telegraph poles and bits of railway line, and was about to collapse at any moment. There was a vast, rusting modern agricultural hangar big enough to park the space shuttle. There were towering corrugated sheds. The farmer had sold his cattle some weeks before and the whole place had ground to a halt: slightly eerie. There were sheep out in the fields in the middle distance – the fields were rented out temporarily to a neighbouring sheep farmer – but the buildings were in decline and obviously had been for some time. I still meet people from time to time who say, 'Oh yes, you live on the heath, don't you? Well, we looked at it, you know.' Too big. Too complicated. Unmanageable. Impractical. And shake their heads.

* * *

It surprised me, actually, quite how nasty it all was, now I was faced with it alone: asbestos, concrete clamps and slurry pits, no garden to speak of. There was the remains of a walled garden, but it was completely derelict now, just a red brick wall remained. Toppling half-demolished sheds obscured every outlook. There was a concrete slab as big as a football pitch just outside the back door, and the back door didn't lock. There was no lock on it. If you approached the house from the right direction, you could just let yourself in. It was a long way from Covent Garden. I didn't know places like this still existed.

As well as buildings there were heaps. The place was characterised, really, by its heaps. Heaps are a feature of farms, just as much as hedges and cows are. Where there is a farm there are always heaps. There were piles of logs, piles of sacks, piles of manure – the farmer had emptied out the old slurry pit and made an enormous cowpat. That was one of the biggest heaps. I wasn't sure what it was but my natural inclination was to climb it. It was a magnificent five-storey whopper. I began to scramble up the side, but two steps in, I was up to my knees. A crust had formed, but underneath it was still very sloppy and warm. It was like a pie. A pie made from the accumulated mess of twenty years of intensive cow farming.

Inside the sheds were piles of bricks, pallets of Cotswold stone, many different species of roof tiles, doors, boards, and timbers divided into oak, elm and pine. Farmers have always managed to recycle just about everything. Apart from old tyres. No one has thought of a use for old tyres, but farmers still tend to hang on to them, perhaps because they know that time will come. There was another, newer pile, which seemed to be horse related. This was fresh, and quite obviously still in business as a pile, still steaming. The farmer and his wife kept horses and had housed them at the farm until the last possible minute. Maybe they'd ridden off on them that very morning. There was a big mountain of rubble next to the horse manure and that was clearly my best pile. There was enough rubble there to make me feel confident. It was reassuring just to have so much of something all in a nice pile. Even rubbish. It wasn't very pretty to look at, that one, but I climbed to the top and everything else looked pretty from there.

You get heaps when there's building work going on, and there always is on farms. Farm is another word for a building site. The first building gangs were actually farmers. Farm workers built barns in the winter months when there was not much farming going on. Actually, stuff pretty much just grows by itself anyway. Farming really means taking care of everything else. That's the tricky bit. There is always something leaking, falling over or blowing away on a farm, and building, rebuilding, patching and fixing are a continuous cycle.

There was a great view of everything from the top of my heap of rubble. I had a good look at the house. It stood right in the middle of the piles of muck, debris and ugly modern concrete slabs. Although it needed new windows you could tell it had started out, and remained, beautiful to the core. The Cotswold type of house is a beautiful thing.

Built to last, built with stone and roofed with stone. Stone roofs held in place by great timbers from woods nearby and from old ships that had once sailed the oceans, now come to rest. The stone roof slates were a mosaic of a million greys, practically alive with moss, and gold and silver lichen, a part of the landscape. It had been built with care, and from where I was standing the roof looked like a work of art and emphasised the sense of shelter a home provides. There it was.

The house didn't look in too bad shape. It was a typical rambling farmhouse with rooms and corridors everywhere, apparently at random. Plaster was coming away from the walls in places. Without the plaster, you could see that some of the beams were maybe a little bit rotten. Now I considered it, the roof looked like it probably needed replacing. The walls were good, mainly, apart from the damp, which made them smell. We'd more or less have to rebuild the whole house, I thought, as I stood there.

The picture was clearer from above. From my vantage point on top of the pile in the stillness, the wonderful whirring silence, I could take it all in. I suddenly felt slightly overwhelmed by my new life. I'd been here a few times but it was only from up here that the scale of the place became apparent. The red brick wall showed there must have once been a garden, as I thought. There were three courtyards of stone stables. The courtyards were all completely unexplored. They were kind of bundled in with the house. They'd all have to find some kind of use eventually, but for now they stood in ruin. I tiptoed over to the other side of the pile to check over the roofs. I knew the roof is always the first thing you have to take care of. As long as the roof is OK a building can sit there for years. The roofs were bad. I knew that anyway, I just thought I'd check. There were holes in all of them, except one stable with a clear plastic roof right next door to the house. It was full of plants and flowers. There was a pond in that room too, with goldfish in.

I slid down the pile and headed for the overgrown tangle of garden. I might never have known, as I know now, that at one time the farm had several gardens. I only found out because of an elderly lady who came to visit a short time after we arrived.

Tiny and delicate, pretty and frail as lace, her eyes darted everywhere. I'd hung on every word she'd said. She told me she was born in the bedroom, and she was still interested in the farm as if it was a person she had once been in love with. 'Oh, there was such a lovely nuttery in that meadow.' She talked about playing in vast orchards behind the walled flower garden and a kitchen garden, which was now completely extinct, concreted over in fact. There had been a tennis court. In one of the fields there had even been a cricket pitch, complete with a pavilion. I've been trying to find that cricket pitch ever since.

As it was now, it was like I'd stepped out of time: a hundred creaking empty rooms and a garden that had been asleep for a hundred years. It was a ghost ship in the sleepy spell of late summer. In the forgotten overgrown corner of the garden, I had to remember to keep my mouth shut when I was walking around to stop flies going in. There seemed to be so many different sorts. The air was thick with them. I swallowed several, which was so horrible it made me shout out loud. It was beautiful, too, but we never shout out loud for beauty when we are alone. Not normally. I was so excited. I shouted. I knew no one could hear. It was breathtaking. Oxeye daisies, those really big tall ones, stood absolutely motionless and inexplicable in gold, waist-deep grass. In the shady corners, the concrete slabs of the old bull pens were being colonised by a creeping moss. There's nothing like moss. It exists at a different scale to the rest of the world. I got down on my knees to look at it more closely. The spiralling chaos of the tiny shoots spoke its own strange language. It seemed to communicate directly with the part of the brain that deals with roofs, and told it not to worry. The top ten most wanted enemies of the gardener had all set up shop and were all looking quite magnificent. There was a thistle rising to head height in full flower. Sticky willy, ivy, granny-pop-out-the-bed and nettles, the charging cavalry of English undergrowth, had been waging war all summer long but now territories were established, and there was a sense of balance and bounty that formal gardens lack.

The superficial silence resolved into the whirr of a myriad living things. There were butterflies and blue tits. There were rooks and rats. The farmer and his wife had shipped out to Stow-on-the-Wold some weeks earlier just leaving the horses so the house was unlived in. Unlived in by people. Everywhere had something living in it. Birds were all over the place like a gas: innumerable different sorts, from tiny whizzing whirling ones to big gliding bombers. I know now that you can always hear birds singing here, but you don't always notice them. It's the opposite of traffic noise. Calming. There were toads under flowerpots. Untold numbers of rabbits bobbed around. The place was empty but ringing with life. I was surprised to see a lizard. I thought they lived only on rocks and in jungles. This one was on the wall in the shade. The insects were much weirder than I had bargained for. A wasp as big as my thumb appeared, angry that I had shifted the balance as I beat a path through the tall grasses.

I was completely alone in deep silence. No taxis. No shops. No cappuccino. No adverts. Just space and peace, and it was all right. I wandered further from the house. The afternoon air was heavy with haze and buzzing. I turned this way and that way, wandering dazed and blissful around another blind corner of the slumbering afternoon. Suddenly there was a blackberry bush as big as a bus, festooned over some hidden banister of shrubbery, decorated with fruit, as festive as Christmas and about twice as delightful for being completely unexpected. I caught an overpowering biff of blackberry smell and it was like being shunted by that white van, now a long way away. Just an hour and a half from London, but another world. I've since come to appreciate that stumbling on unexpected black-berry bushes in full fruit, especially when slightly out of breath, is one of the great delights of nature; a sensory sensation, a smell like a magic spell. Close eyes, deep breath. Better than drugs or dreams.

It was a magnificent spectacle. I'd hardly given black-berries a thought since I was ten. I'd spent my entire adult life in cities. My dad was a fanatical blackberry picker and we used to go all the time when I was a kid, but I'd never, ever seen a bush like this on any of those happy expedi-tions. And there it was, deep in the countryside in the deepening afternoon sun: the quintessential specimen of English flora at its zenith. Overlooked, the bramble. The leaves, a shade of green seen nowhere outside English woodland; the black and red berries, almost psychedelic. I had to stop because of the smell more than anything. I hadn't ever smelled anything like that. Well, maybe when I was a child. All you can smell in cities is drains and food and exhausts. I was transported back to my childhood the moment the first blackberry juice ran down my chin. I stood ecstatic, beyond time. The overgrown garden seemed suddenly to be a kind of Tudor scenario. I stood there smil-ing, chewing blackberries, half expecting Henry VIII to ride around the corner.

I was surprised then, to find a fig tree. I thought that like lizards, they only grew on desert islands. Now I look forward to warm figs from the vine every year in the way I used to look forward to playing in New York City. Figs soften the blow of the end of summer, with their biblical glamour and intriguing insides. I had a rustle around in the friendly boughs expecting to find they were all still as hard as walnuts, but they were soft, ready. I shared them with the wasps.

If César Ritz had surprised me with an unexpected breakfast in bed, I couldn't have felt any more elevated than I did as I wandered into the apple trees. I didn't even know there were any. Orchards are enchanting places. Eden was an orchard. There were maybe a dozen trees standing in patient, orderly rows, bursting with bonsai vigour and laden with fruit. So very pretty. I laughed out loud as I pulled a dangling apple from one of those boughs. I felt in touch with something very big and benign.

In shops, apples all have to be exactly the same size. Shops would probably prefer it if apples were cube shaped so they could fit more in a crate, but I soon discovered that the small ones are the best. They are cuter and they are sweeter. There were four different kinds of apple in the little orchard and they were all as different as cheese and onion and salt and vinegar. There was a mist on the cherry-red skins. I've since learned it's natural yeast. I polished a red one to a deep purple shine on the corner of my shirt.

The joy of fruit trees is profound. They need very little looking after. All they require is the odd haircut. No primping, feeding or weeding. Every year, they bounce back and knock me over with their bounty.

Full of apples, I wandered over to the giant sequoia, the vast tree that dominated the landscape, to see the sun go down. The giant sequoia is the largest living thing on the planet. There's quite a well-known photo of one with a road going through the middle. They come from north-west America, but are fairly common in this country. Great avenues of them line the drives of stately homes like moon rockets, skewing the scale of everything. You see odd speci-mens in parkland dwarfing the ancient oaks. The farmer had told me it was supposed to be the tallest tree in Oxford, but he may have been mistaken. For starters, it's clearly not in Oxford, Oxford is twenty miles away, but it is definitely tall, visible for miles around, straight and narrow as an arrow but leaning gently to one side. It set the tone for the whole farm really, that wonkiness. You could never be too precious living in the shadow of a vast, beautiful and lopsided tree. It towered over everything. I thought it must be hundreds of years old, but it turned out to be a mere sapling. There was one planted on each of the farms in the neighbourhood in the twenties. They can live for up to two and a half millennia but this was the sole survivor. They get struck by lightning and fall. If this one fell on the house it would be all over. Although it was leaning away and pretty unlikely to topple in the wind, it was hard to say what might happen in a lightning strike.

I gradually came under its spell as I stood there. I love that tree. It's the first thing I look for when I'm coming home, the first thing I see when I walk out the front door. It swayed in the breeze. It's swaying in the breeze now. Some people came round a few months ago. They said they wanted to tell me that the man who planted the tree had died, but I think they were just being nosey. I wanted to say

'That's a shame, I would have liked to ask him why he planted something that will be as large as the Eiffel Tower one day, quite so close to my house,' but I managed to contain myself. It was puzzling why this colossal thing had been plonked on the doorstep. There were so many other places it could have gone. That was the perfect spot for a magnolia, not for a Tree-Rex. So many of the problems faced by farmers now are due to that kind of short-sighted-ness in previous generations.

I'd put my marker down on two hundred acres of England, but I still wasn't clear exactly how big an acre was. Very few people seem to know what an acre is any more. Even the estate agent couldn't help me there. Someone had told me Soho was about 140 acres, but it was part of a different planet. Here I was. Alone and quite liking it. I drifted across another huge concrete slab – it was instantly clear how much farmers love concrete – but beyond the huge tiles of the cast concrete pads, tessellating meadows and fields, so inviting: all that space, after being cooped up in a city for so long. I was totally, utterly, completely and blissfully clue-less about farming; about building, about animal husbandry and gardens. Hedging, ditching and dry stoning all sounded like medieval forms of capital punishment. But the idea of having some land to play with was just enough to stop me being scared of what I'd done, which was to cash in all my chips for a vast ship that had foundered, run aground and, however magnificent it was, was beginning to sink.

I spent the days wandering the land, and the evening hours gazing at old drawings of the farm buildings and maps. The farmer had handed me a battered document folder full of well-thumbed drawings and plans stretching back a hundred years or so. There was also a map showing what the parish looked like a hundred years before that – almost exactly the same as it does now: it had the same field boundaries, the same roads and paths, even the ditches and drains were the same. The village was all there and just the same size. It was obvious just from wandering around though, that the valley had been under cultivation for millennia. There were a couple of fields of 'ridge and furrow', the remains of the farming system of the Middle Ages. There was an 'S'-shaped field. When a field is 'S'-shaped, it means it was ploughed by oxen so it would be very old indeed. There were ancient tumuli, standing stones and even one or two lesser known stone circles from the mists of time dotted around the parish. The oldest part of the farmhouse was the bit right next to the well and was probably built as a game-keeper's cottage deep in the Wychwood Forest in the 1600s – I loved the way no one knew. There were wells all around the barnyard. Every time I dug a new hole, I found a well – they are still turning up. I found another one just last month: wells and drains, everywhere. The architecture of the farm wasn't just the stuff you could see. There was lots of stuff underground, too. It had proper sewers that, fortunately, all seemed to be working perfectly.

I'd bought a knackered cattle farm, but a hundred years ago when it was a small part of a vast feudal estate, it would have been knocking out a bit of everything. There would have been chickens, geese and ducks. A pigsty. Back then, it was home to a notable Shorthorn dairy herd. There would have been sheep for wool and for meat, as well as the extinct nuttery and the long gone orchards. A few dozen people would have worked here, taking care of the stock and tending arable crops: fodder for the animals, as well as cereal crops for the household and for market. There had been a bakery – I found the traces of the huge old bread oven, a sooty shadow on a wall – and a dairy that would have produced cheese and butter. Basically, it would have created more or less everything you can find in an upmarket delicatessen in Islington.

Over the last hundred years agriculture has changed beyond all recognition. Within living memory, fields were all ploughed by horse-drawn equipment: now it's all about space age technology; combine harvesters linked by computers to satellites. Farms used to produce a wide variety of crops, but recently farmers have tended to concentrate on just doing one thing – watching machines. There are fewer farm workers and the countryside is peppered with beautiful, but redundant farm buildings. It's easy to make stuff grow, but it's very hard to make money from farming.

Even vegetable gardens, once such practical things, have become quite whimsical luxuries. In terms of cost, it really doesn't make sense to grow your own vegetables. Allotments are popular but no one grows their own to save money. They do it because they like it.

* * *

I suppose I was coming at the place from a different perspective than anyone who had ever worked here, seeing its resources from a tourist's point of view, with a sense of wonder at all the stuff that had accumulated as the wheels of agriculture had begun to turn faster and faster. I hired someone to help, a farm manager, but he clearly thought I was mad and left after a week. I continued poking around and turned up all kinds of treasure. I found a steel chopper, a scythe, in an old shed, it was rusty, but beautifully made and the blade, when sharpened, was the finest piece of steel I've ever seen. I didn't find the old cricket pitch. But after a bit more poking around I did find the remains of a motte and bailey in the railway field – a Norman castle. It had just been sitting there quietly all along.

There was a river. I'd asked the farmer if there were fish in it. He said he thought so but that he'd never had time to go fishing. This seemed crazy. The river frontage was one of the main reasons that I bought the farm. What a thing to have! A river. There was about a quarter of a mile of the Evenlode. It was soon obvious that I would never have time to go fishing either, but the river was a source of hope, the only thing that really seemed to work in the whole place – the only thing I could trust to do what it was supposed to do and not break down, fall over or need servicing. It's been rolling happily down the border of the farm for centuries and will do for centuries to come.

There was a railway line following the river and an eight-acre wood backing on to the railway line. Eight acres of ancient woodland: eight city blocks of the European equivalent of tropical rainforest. Giant puffballs, strange toadstools, thriving in the tangle and orchids, among the remains of rusting pheasant pens, a big pile of green tyres and a mess of rooks. I only found out for sure it was ancient woodland later but the very first time I fought my way in there, it was clear it was primordial. To enter, was to step inside another world with a slightly different climate. Even at the end of a hot summer, in places it was still really quite boggy among the oak trees. The place hadn't been cultivated for decades, hadn't been touched. A dashing hare, a dancing weasel, but no people had been in there for years.

The last few owners had more pressing concerns. Even the farmer before the one I bought the place from, had been chasing his tail. He'd chopped down fifty acres of ancient woodland but there was still a handful of the old forest left. He must have known it was vital. And it was. It was smaller than it had been, but once inside it felt like it went on forever and there was nowhere else in the world; a bit like when you're in Selfridges.

I was used to being one of a crowd. I rarely spent much time alone. The more it was very still and very quiet, the less I seemed to notice I was on my own.

I'd been on endless loops of world tours – passing through hotel rooms, ballrooms and bedrooms – but now I felt anchored to something. The river, those woods and fields, but mainly to my wife. I loved her. It was a combination of things that brought me to a standstill, snapped me to my senses. As a travelling man, I suppose I led many lives simultaneously and didn't take any of them particularly seriously, but now I got to work, thinking with all my might: new home, newly wed, new job. There were a lot of puzzles to solve. My friends all thought I had gone mad, and I had. Love does that. Every shed was a new possibility and for the first time in my life, at the age of thirty-two, I began to get out of bed early. I was always busy. I became absorbed by everything about the place, even the weather. I spent the evenings researching wind speed gauges and rainfall indicators as the heat of the summer began to disperse. The colours changed, and the supreme calm of late September cast its spell over the farm as the haze of summer gradually cleared. The distant horizon emerged in sharp focus and I could glimpse stately homes on their hilltops. The whole landscape softened, all the hard edges obscured by seeding grasses and haywire shrubs. Those derelict buildings full of birds, butterflies and dragonflies, silver sunlight and long shadows, standing still in a strong breeze. The leaves on the fruit trees were starting to droop, yellow and drop. While dawdling in the garden I spotted, picked and ate a solitary apple – a real beauty that had been missed, high up, hidden by leaves until just then. It was only a couple of weeks ago that high summer had its moment, but the blackberries now seemed to belong to a different world, another time and place altogether. Other than that apple and a few cheerful bright jewels of alpine strawberries, there was just the pear tree with its bounty still intact, dangling from almost bare branches, like upside down balloons. The garden party was over.

It was the very last firework of summer, that pear tree. It's miraculous really. I was sure that, like the rest of the garden, it had had little or no attention over the year, or years past. But it was spectacular. I've never had pears quite that juicy.

A fire burned in the grate as I picked every last one, a great big basketful: all shapes and sizes, some long and thin like sausages, and some almost completely round, like dumplings, but somehow still all very clearly pear-like. I couldn't resist eating the little tiny ones while I was out there. The biggest nobbly ones we sliced, seasoned, sloshed with oil and roasted on the fire. Eating them with sticky fingers in a silent huddle, feeling the little kicks in Claire's tummy, watching the flames and listening to the rain as the wind rattled the windows.

And that was it. All of a sudden, snap, the nights drew in. A cold wind rolled in from the east. The lawn was a carpet of leaves and broken rose petals. We'd been living in the garden as much as the house, but from now until the spring we'd be holed up in the draughty house.

CHAPTER 2

SOME PEOPLE AND ANIMALS

Personally, the transformation from metropolitan hell-raiser to quiet country gentleman was one thing, but this was also a professional *volte-face*. I'd bought a business as well as a home.

Playing the bass in a rock and roll band for a living is probably the easiest job in the world. You'd be hard pushed to find a bass player in an internationally successful rock group who'd disagree with that. On the other hand, you'll never hear farmers say anything similar about their line of work. No one says farming is easy, and the rusting super-tanker of a farm I'd taken command of was already threatening to drift over the horizon.

The whole thing was moving. Ever so slowly, moving. It wasn't a house. It was a machine. It was a little bit alive, and things happened even when no one was making them happen. I had no idea what the machine was really, where it started or ended, how to drive it or what to point it at, and I don't know what would have happened if I hadn't met Paddy.

I thought I was doing something quite drastic, quite daring, moving to the country but now I think about it it's quite hard to call to mind an ageing rock gentleman who doesn't live in the country on a farm. The farm is probably the closest thing the ageing rock gentleman has to a natural habitat. As it became clear just how much it would cost to fix the place, and how much there was to know about this world, all of it completely new to me, it was reassuring to think how many of my peers also lived on farms. And it's not just rockers. There are always statistics saying no one wants to be a farmer, but it's the first thing Formula One champions, lottery winners, and movie moguls and billionaires do, as soon as they get the sniff of a chance. Even princes buy farms and none of these people know anything about farming until things start leaking and falling over, and by then it's just too late. They're already hooked.

In the way that rock bands have managers to take care of business, anyone who lives on a farm but isn't really a farmer, needs an expert to call upon for advice on the practicalities. Whether the farm is falling down or a tidy business, there are always lots of those. Things you just don't consider when you're on a picnic: fences, ditches, thistles, trees, frogs. There's a reason why they are all exactly where they are. They've either been put there by somebody, or they live there, or they've escaped or invaded. The country-side is a carefully managed environment. And at the very top of the food chain is the land agent.

Paddy is my land agent. It would be hard to conceive of someone who would fit the bill of English Country Gentleman more perfectly. Educated not far from where I grew up, but in a parallel universe. The product of good genes and a good system, a county-level rugby player and a man able to cope in any situation the world might throw at him. A man of grace and impeccable manners. A keen shot and an excellent rider, he also has a beautiful wife who adores him and a dog who is crazy about him. Everybody liked Paddy and he worked very hard. He was very discreet about his other clients, but I know he built Madonna's stables for her. I'm always disappointed by the lack of imagination of the fantastically successful. They always seem to want the same things as everybody else. There are so many other things to be had. A stable block is so run of the mill. Stables are usually the first thing rock wives go for when they arrive in the country, and are a piece of cake for a seasoned land agent. Paddy and I have had many conversations about stables. We got as far as laying a sort of sub-base layer for a riding school. Claire would have liked stables, but I kept getting distracted. Distracted, constantly overwhelmed by dreams of things that were more interesting and actual things that were much less interesting: the cellar flooding in the middle of the night; sheep escaping and eating the flowers; roofs blowing away. Even the river didn't take too long to burst its banks.

We met every week and I looked forward to it. I always had a long list of questions for him. What is DEFRA? When is the latest we can plant fruit trees? What is the deal with bees? What is the best way to find a cricket pitch? One week I said, 'I want a runway.' He didn't flinch. He said 'That'll be about £150.' Paddy took everything in his stride. Things started to move but the giddying sense of the endless possibilities of a piece of land was constant. There were quite a lot of experts. 'Farm' is another word for a building site, there is a lot to know about building. It is all quite simple, but there is a lot of it and it all happens simultaneously and it is all quite expensive. There are two ways of learning about building. You can go to college for seven years and study architecture or you can use your own money and learn very quickly. Even if you decide to employ an architect you have to know what's what, because if you asked any leading architect for an apple he would sharpen his pencils, draw an orchard and charge you twenty grand. And that would probably still only get you to the planning stage. An expensive architect will save you the most money, but the only way to ever save money is by spending more money than you wanted to in the first place, so any kind of architect is always the start of a slippery slope.

As we rebuilt the house I learned on the go, sometimes at tremendous cost, all the practicalities of plumbing, heating, wiring and flues. I learned about insulation and hardcore and U-values, and all kinds of building regulations, and planning permissions and licences. It was endless and Claire and I would argue about what kind of taps we wanted: polished nickel or satin steel. It was always the ones that were a bit more expensive, that were just a little bit nicer. Soon I had lost interest in taps but became quite fascinated by plumbing systems and water pressure – everything that happens before the taps. They don't really ever manage to make you feel good about yourself, posh taps, not in the way the posh tap brochure tries to make you think they will, but water gushing out of a leaky system like a fountain always lifts the spirits somehow.

We got a couple of pigs without really giving it much thought. I suppose they were the complete opposite of posh taps – pigs were, for hundreds of years, the marker of the peasantry. Actually only very posh people keep pigs any more. Once we'd had them a couple of weeks, it was clear I was spending quite a lot of time with them, more time than was absolutely necessary. 'I'll just go and check the pigs are all right,' I'd say to myself, about twelve times a day. They are very engaging animals, pigs. The quality of contentedness that emanates from the pig as he goes about his business really rubs off. They were just so comfortable in the stable. I made them a nest in the straw and they snuggled up in the corner.

The man who I bought them from had said that the straw I was using was far too good for pigs as soon as he saw it. He rolled his eyes, 'Waste of money,' he said, and he never looked me in the eye after that. An hour after he'd left he sent a text message saying, 'DON'T GIVE THEM NAMES OR YOU WON'T BE ABLE TO EAT THEM!' I settled on 'The Empresses'. I tried to get them to play football, which someone had told me they enjoy, but they much preferred playing with apples. Apples were their favourite thing. They chased the apples round, nibbling at them. They were both gilts, young sows, and they clopped around elegantly. Their dainty knee-lifting gait gave an overwhelming impression of femininity and ballet. The trotter is a similar design to an impossibly vertical high heel. Maybe that's what it was.

As soon as the pigs arrived we stopped having to throw food away. This is a small thing, but one that made me far happier than proportionally it should have. Leftover baby food and sloppy old salad are two of the most redundant things in the universe. You can't use cooked food for compost, really. It encourages rats. So it just hangs around, clogging up the feng shui in the fridge. Those snorkers opened the channels of free-food flow. They transmogrified the guilt of throwing food away into the pleasure of giving. 'Ooh the pigs'll love that,' I'd think to myself. A sack of sprouts going yellow. Yummy. Soon there was nothing going wrinkly in the larder at all. Possibly, I began cooking too much, subconsciously catering for the pigs as well.

They grew at a phenomenal rate. When they arrived I could get one under each arm. A month later they were too heavy for me to lift, but they still came and nibbled my feet whenever I went to see them. I took on a part-time farm hand from the village and he put up fences so they could go and live in the woods when it got warmer. He said his grandfather had dug all the ditches on the farm. It was quite exciting having a farm hand. It meant we could get a couple of cows. One of the benefits of living on a farm, one of the big draws, is having a little menagerie. Funnily enough it was the ditches I was most excited about.

It was pouring with rain. How beautiful it was in the rain, how quiet. A deer bounced over a thicket and disappeared. Paddy and I were trying to work out whether it was the hedges or the ditches that were more desperate for attention. The land was in a pretty sorry state. There wasn't a single ditch that didn't need dredging or a hedge that didn't need laying. We were scratching our heads and stroking our chins when Paddy pointed and shouted 'Racing pigeon!' It didn't look in too much of a hurry. It looked just like the other pigeons, but it did have a tag round its leg. Paddy told me he can always spot them since he'd shot one once by accident, and had felt very bad about it; so bad that he'd sent a note to the address on the little tag saying, 'Sorry, your pigeon died'. 'Delicious, though,' he added. When I lived in London, pigeons drove me mad. I hated the things. When one flew into the farmhouse we were all spellbound. In London I would probably have called the fire brigade, or Rentokill, but this one was so beautiful I wanted to let it stay: all rippling greens and silvers. What a frame, the English countryside! What a lens!

I was changing. I was developing permanent rose-tinted specs. I thought the pigsty was beautiful as well. While Paddy and I tried to put the farm back together after twenty years of chemical fertilisers, poverty and neglect, I rented out the fields to Fred and Gwynne, the local sheep farmers. One of the mothers at nursery asked me how many sheep I had, and I realised I had absolutely no idea. I could tell she thought I was mad and couldn't wait to tell all the other mums.

There was always so much going on, and people asking questions about everything, that I had an unspoken special arrangement with Fred, where we just waved at each other and smiled. He never asked me any questions, and I never asked him any.

I went down to the muddy patch where Fred and Groves, the farm hand, loitered about. 'How many sheep are there, Fred? It's a bit embarrassing, someone asked me the other day and I didn't know.' He didn't know either, I'm sure of it. 'It varies, Alec, you see,' Groves agreed. I could tell, that was what he was thinking, too. I wish I'd thought of saying that, it's a good answer when you've got no idea what you're talking about. I wasn't buying it though. You could say that about the price of bread and still have no idea. I mean everything varies apart from the speed of light in a vacuum. I pushed hard for an answer, which was really outside the terms of our no hassle arrangement. 'Varies between what and what?'

'Four or five hundred, probably, see, now, then there's lambs to come. Then there's Gwynne's as well, see. He'll have a few too.' It was as close as I was going to get to an answer. Gwynne was a quad-bike-riding Welshman shaped like an enormous baby, with huge woolly sideburns and a dog that seemed to be called 'Bastard'. He had some of the fields, too, but it was Fred who did all the waving.

'Talking of sheep, how did it go at Moreton, Fred?' Moreton Show was the regional agricultural event, held yearly.

I had no idea, I had nothing to compare him to, but Fred was evidently some kind of genius. He'd swept the board, won all kinds of prizes. I thought his was the best lamb I'd ever eaten, but assumed it was just one of those things that happens, like thinking your own children are special. It was the right way to think, but I certainly didn't expect anyone else to agree.

Even though it was excellent lamb, it was still really hard to sell. That lamb was all we were producing, in tiny amounts and it was hard to see what else we could do. I stuck at it though and I realised my ambition of making a huge mound out of all the combined piles of rubble. A bulldozer and a couple of dumpers took care of it. I was following a whim really, but I think it's important to follow whims. What else is there to go on? It seemed to make sense to put all the redundant piles lying around the place near the house into one big pile in the distance. I was planning to put a shed on the top and write songs in it, but that big pile instantly became very popular with the sheep. The sheep's quality of life improved no end after the mound. It's not fair to say that sheep are stupid. It is true that sheep don't understand all that much, but they do get mounds. They love them. They were a bit scared of it to start with, but soon they began to flock around it and eventually it was totally mobbed: the only place they wanted to be. They certainly liked the mound more than they seemed to like being organic. They weren't bothered about that at all. In fact they almost certainly preferred to eat junk food. It was very hard persuading Fred to comply with organic stand-ards. Part of the terms of his tenancy was that he would, but he clearly thought it was stupid and I was being conned by someone. He was old-fashioned. 'Maybe we could charge more for the lamb if we sold it as mound-raised lamb,' I said. I've never seen such happy sheep. It can be hard to relate to sheep, but I felt united with them, in our common interest in mounds.

Neighbours are different in the country. They live further away for a start. In London, until I met the neighbours, I thought I had the nicest house in the world. I had been at number 23 for two weeks feeling very good about myself, when I ended up one evening at Dave Stewart's place, which was on the corner of the street. He had excavated some kind of huge spaceship into the rock face of the West End. There were hundreds of televisions, glowing carpets, triple-aspect receptions and a roof terrace big enough for cricket. I was quite miffed when I got back to plain old number 23. Out here, there was one very friendly neigh-bour who came over, and I invited him in for a cup of tea.

He said if there was anything he could do, just let him know. He said, 'We've been wondering how you'd be getting on because, you know, well my father owned all these fields. Mmm. Yeah, but he sold them – had to. They all just kept flooding. Terrible. Terrible fields. Do let us know if you need anything,' and he pulled a sympathetic, helpful kind of face. The weird thing was that I was pretty sure it wasn't true. I couldn't be bothered to look at the deeds. I thought they were the best fields I'd ever seen. The house was coming on well now, too. The Aga was on. There was broadband, all the rest of it, I was feeling like I was doing pretty well for myself all over again. Then one Sunday we were invited for lunch at the pile on top of the hill.

What a house! It was a perfect Gothic castle with ramparts, the endless dry-stone wall and sculptures in the garden. I think it had its own cathedral or I certainly glimpsed something like that from one of the upper windows of the main house. You can really relax in a castle. You feel safe. There was another guy there, and he evidently had an even bigger house. In fact I think he might have had a whole country somewhere or other. It was so nice to get my building problems into perspective, and to talk to people who knew about roofs. In London, people know nothing about roofs. They avoid them. In the country, the more important you get, the more you have to know about them. They are always on the agenda. It is never inappropriate to bring up the subject. Everyone from farm labourers to lords of the manor has an interest in all aspects of roofs, from beam to tile. The two most hotly debated roofing materials were asbestos and, most of all, Stonesfield slates. The stone tiles that cover traditional Cotswold houses were made by frost-shattering the stone. No one makes them any more so all the people who have castles fight over any that come on the market. Roofers offer unsuspecting newcomers good deals on entire new roofs just to get their hands on more Stonesfield slate. Our host said he'd stopped worrying about it and whenever he got a leak, he just popped up there and wiggled something into the hole. He said his grandchildren could deal with it.

Big houses are surprisingly practical. The really massive ones are surprisingly cheap to buy and anything at all you put in a castle looks fantastic. A vast reception hall still looks amazing if all it's got is a sofa that came off a skip and a bare light bulb dangling from some remote ceiling. You can waste so much money on sofas, light fittings and making things look tidy. I'd spent months wondering if I'd bitten off more than I could chew but I came home wanting a bigger house. That castle was historically part of another estate and was numbingly beautiful, but the big house – the demesne of which this farm was once part – is the nicest house I've ever seen. A perfectly proportioned monument: a jewel in the crown of its gardens, which were all laid out by Repton, the first great English garden designer. The estate had once been almost unimaginably vast, a great chunk of West Oxfordshire comprising several villages and tens of thousands of acres, hundreds of square miles. But over the centuries bits had been hacked off and sold as separate titles. In turn, the farm had until quite recently comprised over a thousand acres, with a mill house, several cottages and a campsite which were gradually subdivided into further separate properties.

The campsite, just a small patch of woodland back when it had belonged to the farm, had taken the subdividing process to its logical conclusion. While I was busy planting trees and tearing up concrete, the opposite thing was happening over there. Before I knew what was going on the ancient bluebell wood had been tarmaced and redeveloped into high-class, buy-to-let holiday cabins. The owner tore down ever such a lot of trees and put concrete pads everywhere to receive the pre-assembled executive boxes. It's about as far as you can take the subdividing process: to the high-density luxury level. It really annoyed me that where there had been woods, there was now a lot of concrete. I'd been trying so hard to take things the other way. I was wandering in that direction, and as I walked past the first occupied caravan a very sweet and proud elderly couple were taking delivery of their Jacuzzi; an optional extra when you buy one of these sheds. They looked so content, so fragile. I breathed a huge sigh of relief, and all of a sudden felt my frustration melt.

No matter how far away the neighbours are, it doesn't make life any simpler. All borders were apparently under constant attack, but on the whole I was surprised how much I liked most of the people who lived nearby. Not just the nobs and the billionaires. We took on two gypsies from the trailer park as cleaners and they fascinated me. The younger one was very pretty, one of the prettiest women I've ever seen. She had absolutely no sense of her own beauty. Any number of billionaires' wives would have given everything they had to look like she did but she worked all hours because she was saving up for cosmetic surgery. It was all she talked about. Her older sister had a baby. She brought the baby round one day, dressed from head to toe in heavily branded Armani. She gave us all her Burberry hand me downs. They were kind people.

All was peaceful in the rain. Under heavy skies, the lawn was dotted with bright daisies and buttercups. I'd caught a fleeting glimpse of a moist artichoke and thought it the perfect sight, but it's never perfect for long. I was still admiring the optimistic modesty of the simple buttercup when I noticed a thin trail of translucent sludge coming up through the lawn. I'd never seen sludge like that before. It didn't smell of anything. It looked like aspic. I had to call Paddy. It was everywhere but even he was baffled for once. A couple of months previously I would have been terrified by any mysterious spontaneous sludge phenomena, but I was changing. Worst-case scenario it was just a tiny leak in the space-time continuum. I was sure we could patch it up. But then about a million caterpillar things came out of the lawn and seemed to be making for my shed. They completely ate the lawn. I was trying to write a song and all I could think about was caterpillars. Then I got worried about what they were going to turn into. There were millions of them. There were a lot of slugs around, too, friendly looking things. The more I looked at them the more I liked them, leaving their little shiny trails, the curly graffiti of a strange order. The rain drew them out onto the paths and treading on them as I tiptoed around barefoot at night became something of a hazard. Squish. Ugh.

When you live on a farm, there is nothing, nothing in the world that is anywhere near as interesting, not even pretty faces, as someone else's farm. I went to other farms: dairy farms, beef farms, cider farms, chicken farms, organic poly-tunnel market gardens, fish farms, oyster beds. I spent the afternoon with Jody Scheckter, an ex-Formula One champion. He had the most fantastic farm in the world: vine-yards, the rarest cows in the world, laboratories full of men in white coats and mass spectrometers for molecular soil analysis. He whizzed me around the place at Formula One speed. We stood still in the library for a good thirty seconds, while he pointed at his unique collection of rare books on rare grasses. I needed about a month in there but he wanted to show me the biggest herd of water buffalo in the country. I thought buffalo were mad moose-looking things, but they looked very similar to cows. I think I'd got them confused with bison. Slightly disappointing.

The diversity of farming enterprises was staggering. Llamas and peacocks were surprisingly common in the Cotswolds. There was a big herd of ostriches nearby too. I was about to buy a horse when I began to think maybe I was more of a camel man. Wives are always keen on alpacas. Alpacas look like supermodel sheep, all limbs. They always draw a crowd at country shows but I thought it would be better to stick with traditional animals at our farm, like sheep, although sheep are about as native to Oxfordshire as orang-utans. The Romans introduced sheep and there are probably now more emus and llamas in Oxfordshire than there are in the wild. There isn't much wild left.

Anyway, I had my hands full thinking about earthworms for the time being: Jody Scheckter had made me realise they were much more important than I'd ever given them credit for. Worms are behind everything. That was where everything started, on the worm level. I had noticed that worms don't like lemons. They loved the rest of the compost but always left the lemons. Even worms are more discerning than we give them credit for. They live for ten years and they don't like lemons.

It took a long time to get to the point where we were ready for chickens. You can't really call yourself a farmer if you haven't got chickens. Every farmhouse should have chickens, really. At Moreton-in-Marsh agricultural show you can get everything from little quails to whacking great roosters. We went along and there was the slightly frenzied atmosphere that prevails at these events; there is so much to see and people barge around like in the sales. I was beside myself and dragged Claire, pram and pushchair all around the pigs, cows, sheep and goats before we arrived in the chicken department. I was determined not to leave empty-handed. Prices started at a fiver. It was all quite overwhelming. I said 'Chickens?' to the steward. Forty minutes later, he was still talking, and I hadn't said another word. His message was along the lines of the world of the chicken not being a place to enter lightly. You need to know your requirements egg-wise for starters. There are green ones, white ones, brown speckledies and blue-ish types, plus there are some birds that are good for the table and so it went on. It was so overwhelming that we did indeed leave empty-handed as the place was closing.

Actually chickens are a pure delight and a piece of cake. There is nothing simpler than looking after chickens. There is a book about it but it is quite short and very few people have read it anyway. Keeping chickens is all deliciously obvious. There were already a few pheasants and partridges pecking around the place and doing all right for themselves, so this clearly wasn't a hostile environment for that kind of bird. Pigs are a commitment. They require emotional investment. Chickens don't take much looking after at all, and you'd actually be hard pushed to make a worse job of it than people who do it for a living. So we went to see a breeder and bought some chickens calmly and quietly and I was quite excited. Being a farmer and getting your first chickens, is like being a teenager and getting your first car. I wouldn't like to start working out how much those eggs cost to produce. They definitely wouldn't be competitive on price. I suppose eggs were inevitable, but when the first ones appeared I was stupefied. The longer I stood there, the more spellbound I was by the endlessness of what was playing out before me. Resting on the barn floor, nowhere near the specially commissioned artisan nesting boxes, were one green egg and one brown one. Little cherries on the cake of country living.

I met Daphne because of the garden. She helped me find it and put it all back together. She had her own grouse moor, one of the best in the world. She was quite inspirational, a spritely dynamo granny. There was no holding her back. She was used to dealing with captains of industry and billionaires in her job as a garden designer and she bossed them all around the park, when she wasn't entertaining lord knows who on her grouse moor in Northumberland. We'd walk around the yard, deciding what to demolish. It was always refreshing to spend an hour doing this with Daphne. 'This cowshed, those two old hay barns and that lean-to's days are numbered – knock 'em down,' she'd say. 'They've got to go,' shaking her head and looking appalled, 'They've *got* to go.' Demolishing things is the ultimate expression of freedom. I lay awake at night dreaming of bulldozers, just like I used to when I was a little boy.

Gardens aren't easy. When we first moved here we took advice from a different garden designer to plant a belt of trees behind the garden wall. A tree expert came and planted lots of them. He made a big fuss about them all having to be suitable species. What else did he think we wanted? He was so keen they should be 'suitable'. Then he planted everything far too close together and far too close to the wall. I couldn't have done it more wrongly myself.

Actually it's not wrong to be wrong. It's fine. It's how you learn. I was about to scream at the scale of my own stupidity when it occurred to me that I was actually looking at a row of established oaks that the previous owner had planted. They were also far, far too close to the garden wall. Same mistake. For that matter there was the giant sequoia an arm's length from the front door, the misconception of the owner before that. It was good to know I wasn't the first idiot to live here. I found great solace in the stupidity of my forebears and vented my spleen with Daphne as we battled through the bad planning and planting.

Gardening can go wrong in a million ways. Even when it is going well, home-grown vegetables seem to express themselves more vividly than the ones I'd been used to and they only approximated the shapes, the symmetry they achieved in the shops.

Eggs, though, are definitive eggs. They were surprisingly upmarket. I'd never seen a more accurate egg shape, or a more Farrow and Ball eggshell than those first ones from the chickens. The green one seemed particularly miraculous. I stared at it for ages, pleasantly adrift on a sea of contemplation. I longed to taste it, but I wasn't ready to break the shell quite yet. I wasn't sure whether to cook the thing, hatch it, or pickle it in formaldehyde. However much these eggs cost, it seemed a small price to pay for their mystic perfection and the disproportionate feeling of triumph. It called for a soufflé.

It had really taken a lot of chin stroking and ground-work to get to egg Valhalla. I'd realised by now that farming isn't something you can really rush along and I couldn't see how we could have got to this point any quicker. I knew soufflés weren't easy, but a lot of work would have gone into getting this one to rise. Here's the recipe: first, buy a house, rebuild it, while looking after the ditches and drains, toppling trees, leggy hedges and fallen fences. Begin to convert the entire two hundred acres from intensive beef unit to organic pasture. Next, consider chicken housing, convert a stable and choose chickens. Build more fences to keep dog away from chickens. Take eggs, mix with cheese and place in very hot oven until ready. Voilà! Making a soufflé is simple. Making an egg is the hard bit.

Some things are best homemade. Sometimes, even with no expertise, it's next to impossible to make a worse job of something than the very best, most expensive versions available in the shops. Eggs are probably the best example of this. There is no hen's egg commercially available at any price, anywhere in the world, that would be anything like as good as the worst homemade one. Maybe they are perkier because they are fresher. Maybe they are tastier because household chickens tend to have a more varied diet of scraps and leftovers that would be prohibited commercially. Whatever the reason, eggs from the back garden are in a completely different league from the rest. Of course most people don't have the time or inclination to get involved with chickens. And whatever their shortcomings, shops do make everything wonderfully easy.

The eggs gave me confidence in my farming skills but I still wanted to be an astronaut. I got myself a job in the Astrophysics department at Oxford University. I spent the mornings considering dark matter and the afternoon considering dairy cows. It seemed to make cows much easier to deal with. Cows weigh more than half a tonne and there was something very pleasing about their indisputable 'XXL-ness'. All the equipment that comes with cows is satisfyingly chunky and mechanical too: really big tractors and forklifts. It makes sheep and pig paraphernalia look flimsy. Cows themselves always seem rather pleased with their size and there is a swagger to their parade. Sheep just gambol and graze, they're very low maintenance by comparison. It's a bit like looking after fish and looking at them sometimes made me think I was standing on a kind of seabed, at the bottom of the sky.

I felt the pigs would like me to spend more time playing football with them, but they were quite happy rooting, munching and chasing each other all day. But cows are tricky. There is an extra element of drama in dairy farming because the cows have to be milked twice daily. Margins are very tight in agriculture. Absolutely everything is driven by cost. The modern dairy cow has evolved into something unnaturally skinny with huge udders, a bit like a glamour model. The public tend to assume that farmers are the ones who exploit animals, but it's probably the public who exploit animals by scrimping on how much they spend on milk. I never met a dairy farmer who didn't love cows. You'd have to. Even the ones who were so close to bankruptcy that they couldn't look after their cows properly, loved them.

Most people don't take as much pleasure in cows as dairy farmers. But anyone would marvel at a milking machine. What a huffing, puffing, whirring delight. The best ones are immense rotating carousels which the cows queue up to board one at a time, like passengers travelling first class out of Heathrow. Then they reverse out of the machine and pirouette away – it is almost ballet. The revolving platform holds feeding troughs and udder clamps so that the cows are fed while they are milked. It is an incredibly efficient system but it also manages to give an impression of great spectacle, a benign and mesmerising magic roundabout. I put my name down for a couple of Gloucester cattle. There was a waiting list but that was a good thing. It gave me time to prepare.

At this early stage of my new career, the sheer momentum of livestock was quite hard to deal with. Plants, by contrast, wanted little attention. The fruit bushes in the garden, ignored by everybody in the household, even the new dog, and probably ignored for years before that, seemed to be in better shape than I could have hoped for if they were all I'd ever cared about. And that's the way it is with plants. It's very rare that a plant places demands upon a busy man to make yet another decision.

Of everything, I was most proud of the vegetable garden. It was the first thing that I showed to people when they came round, whether they wanted to see it or not. Plants fascinated me. The plants themselves were under control but the entire garden area was getting bigger all the time, much bigger. The whole blooming caboodle was growing exponentially.

A small stream ran underneath the house, through the cellar. The builders were horrified when they found it underneath the floor. They said, 'You haven't got damp down here, after all. No. You've got running water.' It must have been there since the house was built, so I went with the flow. I left it there. It's been hard to know what to use that room for, though. It is kind of moist. The previous owner had bred his prize-winning fish there, in tanks, so that was an option. I kept empty jars down there because I was planning on doing a lot of pickling. The bigger your house is, the less you throw away. A lot of problems would be solved if everybody lived on farms. Farms produce things as well as consume them, so the motive for recycling becomes quite selfish, a more reliable system. I was taking some old jars down there and as the lights flickered on there was a toad in mid-leap. I nearly dropped my jars. There was a pair of them. It was the perfect place to keep frogs.

Reasons for doing things often become apparent only retrospectively. I should probably have done what the builders advised and tanked out the cellar and made it into a cinema, like all the neighbours have done. But it had all worked out very nicely for everyone concerned. How I would rather watch toads than films, and the children couldn't have been happier than poking toads. A toad cellar probably doesn't add the value that a home cinema would, but I was much more at home with it.

CHAPTER 3

BRITAIN'S
BEST VILLAGE

We hadn't been here very long when John Entwistle died. He was the bass player in The Who and he had lived not far away in Stow-on-the-Wold. I was as surprised to discover he'd lived nearby, as to learn that he was dead. He died in a hotel room in Las Vegas. I thought about him. You could just hear church bells pealing in the haze of the distance if you listened as carefully as you could. It was so quiet and it was just nice, and I wondered how bored I'd be in Las Vegas and what would have happened to me if this hadn't.

I don't think I could ever get bored of this place. It was a bright, infinite, bread and butter midwinter day. Sheep were giving an impression of idleness. Sheep are calming, particularly when seen in the middle distance, nibbling away at the grass. Pigs are at their best close up. They gush with industry and delight. They were always up to something or talking about something to each other. The Empresses had completely won me over and I was putting up more fences, and some pig houses – 'pigloos' – in the woods so that we could get some more. The more pigs there are in the world, the better.

The upshot of the starry-eyed plunge we took when we bought the place on our honeymoon was that I was continually faced with a million practicalities. I don't think we would ordinarily have been bold enough to take such a big step had we not been fresh in love and captivated by each other and the thought of going somewhere new and doing something new. This was where I worked, but first of all it was my home. It was my life.

I worked hard. I got up early. I stayed up late. I rode my bicycle to the village. I still didn't know what the hell I was doing or what was happening half the time, and I missed Blur. Blur were brilliant and I missed being a part of something that good. I thumped through lots of books and I planned agricultural experiments for the coming spring. I discovered tomato plants can grow twenty-eight feet high. I planned orchards. It was possible, with the right combination of trees to have apples in fruit nearly all year. I was getting to grips with roofs and drains, but I still knew nothing about crops, tenancy agreements, single farm payments or swill licences. Actually, I've only just found out I needed a swill licence. I was learning a lot every day and that was what I liked about it.

The nights were cold and dark. I was still a long way from turning the farm into a reasonable business. I was in my shed getting to grips with the elements of English gardens. I'd been reading about forestry all day and I was having a break. It was a really interesting section on pergolas – which I had instantly become a huge fan of. It was just like the first time I heard The Smiths. I was dreaming of making a really long and elaborate bower when the not so pretty gypsy girl came to the door, ashen-faced and said, 'You need to come now. There's loads of ca–cameras, see.' She looked terrified. I could indeed see through the window that there were half a dozen news crews at the front door: cameras, producers with clipboards, runners, make-ups and a gaggle of pretty-but-too-skinny presenters with microphones. I hadn't done a press conference since I got married. I wasn't used to the limelight any more. I wondered what on earth could have happened. Whenever there are that many cameras at the door you assume something really terrible has been discovered. I could feel my pulse in my temples. The fight or flight reflex kicked in. I marched out of the door straight towards them, but as soon as they saw me, all their faces lit up. Every single one of them was smiling. The gods were smiling on us. They all talked at once and wanted to know what I thought about Kingham, the local village, being voted 'Britain's Finest Village' by *Country Life* magazine. I said ahem, obviously we liked it here but I didn't imagine that it is, or even if there is such a thing. I did laugh out loud though and I felt vindicated, just a little bit. I'd never heard of the place when we arrived, didn't even know it was there. I thought this was the middle of nowhere. It had quite quickly become the centre of my world but I didn't expect the rest of the world to notice it. Suddenly it was on the map and it felt like somehow or other we had landed on our feet.

There was a longstanding rivalry between the two neighbouring villages, Churchill and Kingham. For a lifetime, Churchill up the road had had the upper hand: the taller church spire (modelled on the one at Magdalen College), the best swing park (dedicated under-sevens area), and the best pub (The Chequers). But the balance of snobbery suddenly shifted, and they've been ringing the bells at St Andrew's in Kingham a little bit louder ever since. Of course it was all utter nonsense, but the judges were keen on the fact that Kingham had plenty of low-cost housing, as well as mansions and manors. That had struck me too. There was an amazing cross section of people in the village, from rehoused travellers to High Court judges. There is a cricket green at one end and a well-used football pitch at the other. There is a thriving village shop, a school and a troublesome teenager or two, and it was flanked and bordered by land that had been, some of it for many generations, in the hands of grand families: some mad, some bad, some lovely. It was just a little bit real, Kingham. There are villages in the Cotswolds that are among the prettiest places on earth, places that take your breath away. Hidden corners, which can feel more like exclusive islands in the South Pacific, disconnected from the rest of the world.

Kingham is an entry-level kind of paradise with geezers, asbos and greboes. I don't think anyone in Kingham took the matter very seriously, although everyone in the Tollgate Inn stayed late that night, but all the surrounding villages, the ones with better preserved stocks, earlier architecture and more legitimately famous residents were clearly slightly miffed as time went on, and as the place was continually mentioned as the jewel of the Cotswolds. The Cotswolds is snobbier than Paris, snootier than Upper West Side Manhattan, and the residents of Lower Slaughter, which always performs very well in 'Britain in Bloom', or Upper Slaughter, which has a Michelin-starred restaurant, were somewhat taken aback. Kingham could only boast a family-owned hotel that served twelve-course spectaculars in a creaky old silence. I rather like that hotel. There is the British Legion, too, for the geezers. Geezers have very few places left to go now that their natural habitats, pubs, are full of middle-class women drinking rosé.

Even though it is ridiculous to say somewhere is better than anywhere else, there was a serious upshot for the local community. The buoyancy of Kingham's assets made it easier for local businesses to get investment. There was an accompanying redevelopment boom of such proportions that it was impossible to get a local builder. They all remortgaged and went to work on each other's houses. The camping site had already transformed into a camping suite. Our nearest neighbour, a plumber, knocked his cottage down and replaced it with a post-modern eco-castle. The electrician bought a tranche of East Anglia and disappeared.

I took up football again, but here it was played slightly differently. My first Kingham football match was the best I've ever played in. It may not have featured the most skilled exponents of the game, but it was the most fun. It was an old Etonian, an autistic ten-year-old, a passing crusty dogwalker and a nightclub promoter, against the mums, the toddler and me. I was wearing a suit and a pair of GI pumps. The girls were in tight jeans. There was a lot of mud on the pitch, from a tractor driving back and forth, by the look of things, and the chaps had the considerable advantage of the slope. Blackie, who had been walking his dog, was in goal. He said he'd once been the drummer in Hawkwind. He looked like he might have been. He didn't have many teeth left. When he found out what I used to do for a living, he asked if I'd like to join his band. They did Motorhead covers. His family were rehoused travellers. I liked them. His wife taught art at the local comprehensive, and he was on terms with all the nobs in the big houses because their daughter was some kind of genius who had won a scholarship to the top private school in Oxford.

Our fresh young forward, the two-year-old, was causing a few problems but mainly for his own side, as he was constantly wandering off and having to be rescued by one of the team. What a brilliant game football is. I'd forgotten just how much more fun it is doing football than watching it, especially with girls playing. There were frequent bouts of hysteria and a lot of running commentary. Claire, in goal, got a muddy one on the nose from the opposition, which galvanised the team spirit and took the competitive element to another level. The two-year-old found a big puddle that fascinated him and he sat down to play in the mud. Once he had stopped running away we really rubbed their noses in it. It felt good afterwards, the winter sunshine was warm and you could see for miles and miles. Far more people watch football than play it. Watching the best team in the world is nothing compared to playing in the worst. Football made me feel good.

We were nearly ready to decorate. 'Who can paint?' I asked.

'If you can piss you can paint,' said John, slowly and wisely, and everybody cheerfully agreed. We were sitting in the static caravan, me, John – the semi-retired chippy with a lifetime's worth of breaktime wisdom to draw upon – and Blackie and Doa. Blackham and Doa were the only idlers left in the village, or had been until they started working for me. I felt slightly guilty for steamrollering their idyllic lifestyles. They were happy chasing barbel, growing their own vegetables and going to see Motorhead occasionally but due to the buoyancy of the local economy it was no longer possible to live here and not have a job, even if you'd retired. I suppose I thought I'd come here to retire, after all.

I was quite absorbed in village life, but it was surprisingly easy to stay in touch with people I cared about from the past too. In fact getting some distance from everything had helped me realise who I did care about. We were far enough away from London for people to think about staying the night if they came to visit, and even though everyone had said we were mad to do it in the first place, all the ones who had been the most indignant about what we were doing, were the ones who wanted to come and stay now it was Britain's 'Best Village'.

I was living in a different world. Most of the time I didn't have any cash or any keys in my pocket. In the summer I didn't wear shoes. In a way living on a farm was a return to a childlike state. There were far more exciting things to spend money on than comfy chairs or plasma screen tellies: now there were pergolas and gazebos, cherry pickers and mini diggers. I liked the places where they added the VAT on afterwards and sent you a monthly bill: builders merchants and plant hire companies. The countryside is not known for its shops. Stow-on-the-Wold sold fudge and antiques. Bourton-on-the-Water just sold fudge. Most of the villages didn't even have a shop at all any more. I remember going to the country when I lived in London and feeling there was nowhere to spend my cash: it's quite a nauseating feeling, when your money's not worth anything or it won't get you anything.

That wasn't a problem in Kingham, because of Daylesford. The reason people wanted to come to Kingham was because of Daylesford.

*   *   *

I only discovered Daylesford by accident. My dad spotted it actually. Daylesford is the poshest organic farm shop in the world. There are shops I have to go to, and shops I like to go to. Daylesford Organic is one of the latter. More than a farm shop, this is a farm shop so fabulous that it gentrified the whole neighbourhood. It probably added more to the value of houses in the area than having a member of the royal family move in would have done. It really is a spectacular feat of fantasy, realised. Organic principles bundled up with glamour, off pat, tied with a ribbon into a retail experience every bit as sensational as Bond Street or Liberty. It was like accidentally wandering out of the economy cabin of grocery shopping into first class. The place was full of blissful-looking yoga chicks and anxious-looking husbands. The only problem with it, was that it was expensive. But how expensive can a carrot be? I have to say, I don't care how much a carrot is. It can't be that much and if it is really good, I'll pay. Daylesford was incredibly popular with Cotswold high fliers, and a whole scene and mythology grew up around it. People who live in the Cotswolds don't tend to go to other villages. It's like London, people who live in Clapham never go to Camden. But everyone goes to Daylesford. There were credible reports of local movie stars spending thousands of pounds per visit, and aristo-cratic ladies unable to control the frequency of their trips to the holistic massage parlour. To shop there cost the earth, but it was heaven. The place radiated prestige and dispensed comfort.

It was all the dream of Carole Bamford, the wife of a local billionaire. People laughed at her, said she was losing money, that it was a hobby and that it was ridiculous, but somehow she had actually created the most desirable food brand there is. She didn't particularly care about making money. She wanted to make amazing food. That was why the brand was so powerful and so valuable. It was food couture. I could see the Bamfords' land from my bedroom window. I've never seen grass as green as that. It was a bit like the rest of the local countryside, but it was slightly neater and greener, even from a distance you could tell how tidy it all was. Part of the shop's charm is that it was just nestled away in the middle of nowhere: rolling countryside at the heart of the next-door estate. The first time I went to the shop was on a Saturday. People had flocked in from all points west: on foot, on horseback, by motorbike and side-car, in Bentleys and 4x4s. I parked my bicycle between some kind of dragster and a convertible BMW. There was nothing ugly and not a single reminder of any of the bad things about the world, not the merest hint. Even the car park was a beautiful thing, full of other beautiful things.

The renovated farm buildings that housed the shops were beautiful. I realised they were just like my buildings, probably built by the same builders at around the same time, but these had the benefit of a brilliant re-design. The perfect balance of rustic and contemporary. It was like strolling into Belgravia 'en pays'. To enter was to be overwhelmed by a sea of beige punctuated by topiary splodges.

As a rule of thumb you can tell how affluent people are in the Cotswolds by how skinny they are. Everyone was skinny in Daylesford. As I arrived, two latte-sipping gymkhana mums in full regalia – knee-length riding boots, thigh-clinging jodhpurs – climbed aboard their super-charged Range Rover, happily chattering in fluent New Age. I passed a conspicuously gay man in a cravat carrying what might have been a cabbage – or could have been a large, unusual flower – to his car, a pristine vintage E-type Jag. He exuded great hauteur, incredibly managing to suggest that the whole experience was beneath him. And that's how posh the Cotswolds are. There is always some-one who thinks they are above the situation, no matter how spectacular it is.

There is never anything in the food hall that it would not be nice to take home. Once inside it's irresistible, spellbind-ing. Buying food elsewhere is just unthinkable. It's not that cheap, but a crisp paper bag of groceries from there was enough to keep me happy for quite some time. What meats! Everything from snipe to sausages ranged alongside unrec-ognisable vegetables from abroad and perfect specimens of familiar ones fresh from the market gardens right outside. The bread counter was piled high with rye loaves, batons and soda whoppers. There were pastries. There were tarts. There were full-on legs of ham, cheeses I'd never seen before. Everything was beautifully wrapped, perfectly lit and immaculate. There were even copies of *Dazed & Confused* and *Wallpaper* magazine at the checkout. It was all absolutely ridiculous and fantastic and sexy. I spotted a cruising Bentley bachelor who was unable to remember the name of the cheese that he liked, but the man on the cheese counter knew, and he knew the gentleman's name, too.

Daylesford is a place that all women like. At least there seemed to be more women than men there. A lady of indeterminable age, wearing a denim mini skirt and looking very good, whilst rather nonchalantly buying truffles, was talking on her mobile. 'Darling, I'd love to but the Clarksons are coming for dinner and the cook's freaking out again and I've got to go to New York in the morning. See you in LA. Bye, darling.' It was more glamorous than Cap d'Antibes and it was November and we were only thirty miles from Coventry. I was distracted by another lady in her forties in another short skirt–bare legs combo carrying a huge pot of tall flowers, so that I couldn't really see her face. It was a surreal triumph, after Magritte. The whole shop is that. A shop in a field in the middle of nowhere. She was on the phone, too, behind the flowers, talking quietly, probably to her husband, confessing to having just spent all their money on flowers.

Daylesford is a colossal operation, a huge investment and a triumph of the 'if you build it they will come' school. Master bakers, pastry chefs, butchers, wine buyers, and goodness knows what other experts all going at it behind the scenes from dawn till dusk to fill the shelves. I was shown around the area where the cows were milked. The milk was fed directly by a pipe into the hands of an artisan cheesemaker and turned into award-winning cheese on the spot. A lot of the stuff in the shop was produced from scratch, with scientific attention paid to every detail on site, but all the home-produced lines were topped up with the finest luxuries from the four corners of the globe. It was a case study in excellence.

What a business to stumble upon in the Gloucestershire countryside. The food hall was just a part of it. There was a whole New Age massage, yogaromatherapy wing, apparently entirely staffed by Tibetan Buddhist monks offering the latest treatments from facials to full body massage. Alongside the new clothing department, was an interiors division full of knick-knacks and tasteful *objets*. Another building, with roaring open fires and scented candles, sold books about yoga for dogs and other suitable gifts for those who have everything. I took a tour of the market garden behind the shop. I roamed polytunnels full of exotic salad. From an observation deck I watched the cows being milked. I saw the yoghurt and butter-making facilities. I watched the artisan cheesemaker creating his award-winning cheese. They weren't just making cheese, they were making milk and turning it into cheese and they didn't just make milk, they made grass. You could tell worms were being taken into consideration and somewhere behind the scenes was someone who knew worms don't like lemons. A group of wide-eyed Gore-tex-clad tourists looked clearly out of place, wondering at the sheer financial scale of any shopping activity. They stayed in a huddle and nudged each other and pointed at things, slightly scared, but thoroughly exhilarated.

I loved it. It was a dream that deserved to succeed. I couldn't help thinking I was looking at the shop of the future. It did for shops what Ian Schrager did for hotels in the nineties. Made everything that had happened before look boring. Buying the groceries at Daylesford would never be a chore. It was a joy, because Daylesford managed to have that quality of being somewhere that it is actually quite nice to just pass the time. People didn't go there just to buy *filets mignons*, they went to see and be seen. Even the chatelaines of the larger houses liked to drop in to pick up an extra bowl of chocolate-coated cherries when they could easily have sent their cook. It was amazing how it polarised people locally. The pickle factory caused an uproar in the village and was shut down. Many of the locals thought the whole thing was a nonsensical conceit for tourists and never went there. Fred sold lamb to Daylesford but he didn't know what to make of it. He just shook his head and went very quiet whenever it was mentioned.

But it was a magnificent thing to have on our doorstep: as inspirational as it was convenient. I still didn't really know what I wanted to do with my new life, I just wanted something else, but Daylesford was such a sophisticated dream, perfectly realised, that it showed that whatever it is you want to do, however far-fetched it is, it can be done. Right here, bang in the middle of nowhere.

There was always something happening at Daylesford but I was surprised by how much community activity there was, generally. I had no idea there would be so much going on in the countryside. It was one festivity after another in the parish. There was a firework display on top of the hill. It was the talk of the queue in the Post Office. We decided to go, but I had trouble finding Claire's left welly and by the time we left, both furious with each other, with a sinking heart I saw the first firework go pop in the distance. It was all over by the time we arrived fifteen minutes later. We missed that one, but it soon became clear that firework displays would be actually quite hard to avoid. They seemed to be going on all around, all winter long. There were about three thousand people on the village green on bonfire night itself. Some druids performed quite a dark ceremony with a very lifelike guy while we munched burgers, spangled sparklers and watched our children on the bouncy slide. It seemed just as glamorous and interesting as Brook Street, Mayfair at midday or Newcastle in full swing at midnight. The bonfire was enormous and the fireworks went on for ages. Perhaps they never stop. I suppose there's always a firework going off somewhere.

There was a pamphlet that came through the door every month with adverts for curtain alterations and swimming pool maintenance. I couldn't help reading it. I always wanted to call every number in it. One month, between a landscape gardener and a fitness trainer, there was a new number to ring for singing lessons. I thought I'd have some singing lessons. I still played the guitar every day. I was in the best band in the world. I didn't want to start another one, but I clung on tight to music, tighter than ever.

I started having singing lessons on Mondays. And I loved it. I loved it more than I'd loved flying aeroplanes.

Loved it as much as it was possible to love anything. It was about as good as it ever gets. I came bouncing out of that tiny house in the next village every single time, with resolve and purpose, feeling as zippy as a bouncy ball inside a balloon, and I walked around singing all week. It is a leap of faith to sing, like jumping into water. It is a kind of floating. I think the hardest thing about it was to relax and believe I could do it. A little bit of encouragement worked wonders. The teacher played the piano and I sang, Roy Orbison, old rock and roll songs, gospel hymns, we sang in harmony, our voices ringing out across the valley. I was convinced it was the best band I'd ever been in, that one: me and the singing teacher.

Having music lessons was something I'd completely changed my mind about. I'd long had a disregard for musical academia. It wasn't the way I'd learned how to play. I'd learned how to play by copying my dad and it never fitted in to anything that was taught at school. You do have to be careful with these things. They are just as likely to knock you down as build you up. Maybe I was scared of how little I knew. Music was the only job I'd ever really had, but I'd never had a single music lesson. I could tune a guitar without a tuner and that seemed to be all that was required until now. Now I felt a compulsion to study. I once stayed in a karaoke bar for three days, but this was different from karaoke. It was always my turn to go next and the teacher would patiently say things like 'Can you try that bit a bit louder,' as he tinkled along on the piano. He had no idea who Blur were, and I loved it.

I was enjoying singing so much, that when word got round about a drum teacher I thought, what the hell? The drum teacher came to the house. That tells you something about the different mindsets of singers and drummers straight away. There would be no question of a singing teacher coming to your house. Singers, to a man, like the world to revolve around them. Drummers, even the drummers in the world's biggest bands, tend to be basically willing, nice blokes. I was always cancelling the drum teacher at very short notice. The world isn't really fair on drummers. Any record producer will tell you that the most important ingredient of a pop record is the drums. After the tune it's the most difficult bit to get right. Drummers very rarely get songwriting royalties, though. It doesn't make sense. If you can master rhythm you're well on your way. Drums and singing are different like France and Germany. They're part of the same map but everything happens differently. Banging things and screaming and shouting are both very primal. They are small children's two favourite activities. Music is a primal language, and singing and drums are the purest aspects of it. Musical instruments are a bit more arbitrary.

The whole penchant for music lessons had started with Mrs Swann, the piano teacher. At least it started as a penchant. By the time I was having singing lessons it had become a zeal. I started to wonder if I was going mad when I realised I was hankering after a tuba. If I'd seen a tuba for sale, I knew I wouldn't be able to help myself. I started making enquiries about tubas. I was beginning to worry about myself, but I have since discovered that in the classical world many bass players play the tuba. But it all started with Mrs Swann. Her number was in the Post Office window and I went round to see her. We had a chat in her immaculate sitting room. I explained to her that somehow or other I'd been a musician all my life, but I just kept assuming the bubble would burst as I'd just been winging it.

Mr Swann was a legend in the village. He was a hundred years old and he was always immaculately turned out. A man of great height and noble bearing, he took pleasure in answering the door and showing me in every week. He would then disappear into his garage and tinker around with spanners while his wife did her best with me. Mrs Swann must have been in her eighties, maybe even older. She was as delicate as a dandelion clock but razor sharp. She was an examiner for the Guildhall School of Music. She had no children of her own but she had won scholarships for countless local children over many decades. Music was her life. She taught the local headmaster and other dignitaries in the area. I think she had me down as a 'could do better', right from the start. I was always forgetting my book and I always seemed to be just a little bit late. I've never felt so scruffy as I did when I was in that perfectly arranged house. The silence in it was like an enormous ship and I'd slam fat C minor chords at it like a bottle of champagne. Mrs Swann said the biggest challenge was teaching me to play quietly. As she pointed out most weeks, piano actually means 'soft' so it's always worth bearing that in mind. Once you hit a certain age, life becomes one long and sometimes difficult quest for soft, I suppose. By the time she had ticked 'The Entertainer' – the last piece – we had spent a year doing *Book 1*. Even learning how to fly an aeroplane only took three months.

It's difficult. Maybe that's why I'd never wanted to do it before. Maybe it never felt necessary. The engineer's assistant on the last record I made had a degree in music, but in fifteen years of making records, I can't think of anyone else I've worked with who had any kind of recognised tertiary musical qualification. All a singer really needs is a big mouth. Bass players get by on haircuts and grins. Guitarists usually have some idea of what's going on, but not enough to hold everyone back. Keyboard players know the most generally and so are usually best avoided. One guy, who I started to write an opera with, had some sort of drum doctorate. But as he said himself, being a great drummer is not about being able to do anything fancy, it's about being able to do the basics, really, really well, like Martina Navratilova at Wimbledon. That was confirmed by Madness' drummer, Woody. I bumped into him at Daylesford. Daylesford was that kind of place, where anyone might walk through the door. I told him I was having drum lessons. He said, 'You don't need drum lessons, son. No one needs drum lessons. Drums go bum, smack, bum, smack. That's it.' He got me to sing some Madness songs to him and accompanied me with bum smacks. He was absolutely right.

*   *   *

I only met Bill by accident because I live here and so does he. Mind you, that's how I met Graham Coxon, Blur's guitarist. We lived next door to each other as well. I've heard a lot of people play the guitar but I can tell you without even stopping to think about it that the two best guitarists I've heard over the years are Graham Coxon from Blur, and Andy Bell who was in a band called Ride originally and, oddly, ended up playing bass in Oasis. Those two were in a completely different league from anyone else, everyone apart from Bill. Bill is the master. He'd been around for years and he'd played with everybody. In the sixties he backed Motown singers. In the seventies he wrote for Art Garfunkel, and in the eighties he wrote the biggest selling song in Norway, ever, and he went out with Leslie Ash. Now he composes for orchestras and when the Queen and Prince Philip celebrated their Diamond Wedding anniversary, Bill was commissioned to write some music to mark the occasion. He's a dude.

As I was playing the piano and he was playing the guitar one afternoon, I started to think, hey I'm really getting the hang of this piano business. But it didn't sound so good after Bill had gone home. It's the true mark of a really great player to make everyone else sound good. The best way to improve, and it probably goes for everything, not just music, is to associate with people who are better than you. You improve much quicker that way than you ever could on your own. I played a lot on my own as well, though. Guitars just sounded fantastic in the new kitchen, it was a total accident design-wise. I'd spent a lot of money on a new fireplace that didn't work. It smoked whenever the wind blew from the north. It was a disaster but I suppose I could have spent a fortune on acoustic design and not got close to making guitars sound anything like as good as they did by that fire. Bill kept bringing round new guitars just to see what they sounded like in there.

Bill lived in a two-storey hay barn in a hamlet too small to have a name, on a grand estate up the road. His only possessions were three large art books, which he always tried to give me when he got drunk, and about six guitars, one of which he took everywhere with him. He was terrified of flying, but he had to go to Norway a couple of times a year because he was very famous there. I went to Windsor Castle to see a performance of the piece that he wrote for the Queen. It was great, so great Bill bought a dog to celebrate. He didn't drive. He hardly ever went out. I went to see him one bright frosty morning and he was sitting at his kitchen table in the streaming sunlight with a huge piece of manuscript paper in front of him, writing a duet for guitars. It was all in his head and he was sitting there with a neat propelling pencil and a little rubber and writing it all down in the silent sunshine, like he was doing a crossword. It was staggering. He said, 'Well, you know, you don't get much money for writing classical music, but there's only a couple of guys in the world who can play this stuff, and they both want to.' He was very excited about his marmalade, and we crunched toast and I sang him some football chants.

* * *

Lots was happening. Wheels were constantly turning. I was throwing everything at my new life. We were building a garden, renovating the house and barns, turning the land organic and getting to grips with the derelict woodland. Blackie, the grebo, the one who used to play the drums in Hawkwind, and his mate Doa, a White Stripes fan, were stripping out the enormous threshing barn. It was a magnificent structure, that, and I became quite awestruck by the possibilities of building. I loved the idea of building stuff. I wondered if there would soon be a properly famous builder, someone who could win ladies' hearts like singers can. It's not all that long since composers held the same status as builders: tradesmen. Composers became rock stars and builders became distrusted, maligned. But maybe things were changing. The guy who drove the digger on the farm was building a swimming pool at his house. What woman would want to live in a rented barn with a dog, three large art books and six guitars when she could be sitting by the pool with a digger hunk? People who are married to musicians tend to be irritated by their spouses playing their instruments anyway. I remember a girlfriend of Graham Coxon's telling him to leave the bloody guitar alone because she was trying to watch *EastEnders*. I'm sure she wouldn't have minded him putting some shelves up.

I didn't mind not having a car, or an aeroplane. I'd sold the aeroplane. The car was toast. At the moment there was just a couple of bicycles. I could do all my local business on the bike. I only really went to the Post Office, Bill's, Daylesford and Mrs Swann's, for piano. I got the train to

Oxford. I sacked the singing teacher because he kept cancelling me, saying sorry but something had come up. It was a bit like being ten years old again, zooming around on a bike, feeling a great sense of liberty and having no idea what the future might hold, but that I could make it all up if I was brave enough. Sometimes I liked the mountain bike. Sometimes I took the racer. Riding down a steep hill on a bicycle is one of life's great highlights. It's up there with New York pizza, second gear in a fast car, E minor on a guitar and breakfast at The Wolseley. The bicycle is the best invention ever and the best way to travel.

There was quite a lot of excitement about the quad bike arriving but it was a great disappointment. The tiptronic gears kept getting confused and jamming up. Compared to the flawless, fantastically efficient design of a bicycle, a quad bike is a stupendously bad piece of engineering. It was dangerous, too. There was a fast growing list of high-profile people coming a cropper on their quads. Come to think of it, the quad bike came with whatever the opposite of a celebrity endorsement is; they are more of an occupational hazard for A-listers. It was easy to see why people were mangling themselves. Quads are very powerful and very unstable – the motorised equivalent of famous actresses. Even over flat ground it was hard to handle, and it was full of unnecessary electro-gizmos that broke down if they got wet or muddy.

It broke down straight away. Then Doa lost the keys and by the time I'd got some more cut, the battery had gone flat. I got a twelve-volt charger from the farmer shop and the gardener hooked the battery up to it in a barn known as 'the bothy'. There were all kinds of barns, they all had names and that one had always been called the bothy. It had a little fireplace and the farm hands used to have their tea in there in days gone by. Now Fred and Gwynne had Range Rovers with heated seats so they never used it. I'd patched the thing up and it was very cosy in there. So cosy, that while the battery was charging the door swelled up in the frame and wouldn't open. The battery was stuck inside, all fully charged until spring. The builders didn't want to take the door off. It was an odd-shaped doorway, and I'd just had the thing made. I bought a new battery but in the meantime Blackie, who understood motorbikes, had taken the whole thing to pieces because he thought the gearbox was making a funny noise. It took him about a month to put it back together again by which time I had lost interest in the whole business. It was a slow motion catastrophe.

I loved my new life in the country, but winter was long and dark and cold and, however beautiful it was, I couldn't cut myself off from the rest of the world all the time. I confessed to myself that I missed the old days, missed being really good at something. In those occasional cup-half-empty moments I was isolated in the country, a half farmer in a half renovated farm and though I was willing to learn, I had to because it was still something I knew hardly anything about. I had met, fallen in love and married my wife in a spin, but what did she really think about it all? She'd married a rock star and she got a crap farmer. There wasn't much I could do about it. Graham wouldn't return my calls and Damon was way too busy. Gorillaz was massively successful and it suddenly looked as if everything clever Blur had ever done was his idea.

One of the pigs died from a kind of pig measles. Claire cried. I was quite upset, too. We couldn't move her, The Empress, anywhere for a while because there was a foot and mouth scare, so she lay in the big shed, going nasty and casting the shadow of death over the place. If it were up to me, I'd have lit the huge pile of deadwood we had gathered from around the barnyard and incinerated her on top of that. It was a big one, a perfect pyre for a pig, with a rotten one-tonne hay bale on the top like a cherry on a cake. She'd have been stylishly vaporised into air and ashes in there. Otherwise I'd have made a big hole with the digger and buried her in the Jurassic stratum of the subsoil, under where the asparagus is going. Unfortunately, both were illegal, so she just mouldered under tarpaulin while death and the law mocked each other.

Death is a downer. It was cold and dark, and the days seemed very short. Still, Christmas was round the corner.

WINTER

CHAPTER 4

COUNTRY CHRISTMAS

Suddenly it was cold, really cold: wet and cold but beautiful. Water everywhere, collecting in puddles, knee-deep in clear pools around farm gates, swelling hidden ditches and working quiet rivers up into torrents. The meadows at the bottom of the valley were gone. Now there was just a huge flat black mirror: the entire landscape transformed, unrecognisable from the week before and full of different-looking plants and animals. Snipe flew up and zigzagged off out of a clump of undergrowth. Midwinter and not a soul in the valley other than startled birds. It was perfectly still, as if it had all been there, unchanged for eternity, all bold primary colours and simple geometry. I thought I'd never see anything as pretty again but then the first hard frost arrived under the spell of a perfect full moon and I woke up inside a Christmas card.

* * *

It was all as festive as a Friday off and I found myself drawn down a muddy farm track with my best shoes on, drinking it all in. There were a million things happening as usual, a million things to do, fiddly decisions to make. No matter how much I did and how much money I spent it was beginning to sink in that it would never get to the point where anything here was finished or even at rest for a moment. A farmyard is a lens, a place where a lot of continuous processes pass into focus and, as the place was in pieces when we bought it, I was still playing catch-up. I was off to meet Paddy to decide which tracks to lay and which gates to replace next. My clean shoe broke through a sheet of ice. I yelped as it went in and groaned as it came out covered in mud but realised I was smiling and no matter what happened, in a way the place was perfect and always has been. An open field on the first day of December, with all the promise and anticipation of Christmas ahead, is a sight for sore eyes.

The clear winter mornings made everything seem closer together: all the confusing detail was stripped from the landscape, neighbouring houses could be seen clean through the hedges that hid them most of the year: exposed, secret-less.

Then suddenly, in the middle of the week and with no warning we had the first proper fog of the winter, a whumping blanket that lingered until after lunchtime, until it got dark again. I couldn't see the garden wall all day. It was as easy as it was pleasing to throw a stick beyond the observable horizon into the infinite mists of forever. The entire valley stilled and silenced apart from the odd nervous car engine in the distance. 'I like it. It's cosy,' I declared to everyone in the kitchen, mainly dogs, but this time of year was an acquired taste. No one else had a nice word for the weather. The chickens started fighting, the sheep were always falling over. The remaining pig had measles, the dog had fleas, tractor, quad bike and digger were all in pieces. Roofs were blowing off, hedges out of control. There were mulberry trees ailing, beams failing, badgers, rats, rooks, rabbits all trying to gatecrash. There was always some small emergency or other unfolding in the tiny soap opera, something that demanded my full attention. The upside was that since becoming a farmer I had noticed that existential angst, the terrible malaise that afflicts all those who have too much of anything, had evaporated completely.

The utter boredom afforded by the riches and misanthropy inherent in international rock stardom had been replaced with different troubles. 'Why?' had gradually turned into 'How?' and that's a much better class of problem to have. I pitied anyone who knew what they were doing. I was at least having a great time finding out whether I'd bitten off more than I could chew. I suppose we were rich when we started. I'd never really thought about money, though. I've come to realise that's probably all being rich is, as good as it gets: not thinking about money. Now there was always something to be built, mended or experimented with. The farm was a money-eating monster. When I was gallivanting around town, George Besting it from one expensive restaurant to the next with a full complement of hangers-on, I had a feeling I was being irresponsible but now I thought about it, that all seemed like quite good value for money. It was quite a cheap lifestyle in comparison to living on the farm. It would have been possible to support a bevy of hangers-on and acolytes for months for the price of fencing a couple of fields with post and rail plus rabbit netting. Living on a farm with an expanding family was far, far more expensive than living in Claridge's like I had done. And now I was getting up early and working late and I hardly ever had breakfast in bed.

Throughout the ups and downs of farmer-hood, the modest triumphs and insignificant disasters, the river, my river, the Evenlode was a constant source of strength. It's a river. It never failed me, never really went wrong. It couldn't. At least even when it did go wrong it sorted itself out again. All I could do was watch. And I loved watching that river, flowing on and on, constant and lovely, pouring with gentle authority towards London, placing me comfortably upstream of my past. It was my most treasured asset, that river, even though it had no real monetary value. Even during the sinking of nearby Tewkesbury one summer, that river was all just fine. Our bank didn't even overflow, although the field on the far side was under water for most of July. Well, it is a water meadow, a flood plain. That's what they do. They flood sometimes. The river was the only thing in the whole place that never presented me with a problem to solve. I couldn't help smiling when I opened a letter from the council saying that in view of the recent very heavy rainfall they were going to come and check the river was working all right. They'd sent a map of the farm with a big red line going down my favourite ditch.

I was changing. The biggest difference was not that I had swapped the city life for one of a quiet country gentleman, that I became a husband or that I had a new job as farmer, but that I had become a parent. Claire had been pregnant the week we moved in and she had been practically ever since. In next to no time we had become quite a large family. A band is a bit like a family: that was what made it hard being estranged from each other to begin with, because I think from the moment I met Claire, the band stopped being my family. When the band disintegrated I'd lost my job, my hobby and my family all in one go. I didn't speak to Graham or Damon for months at a time but every year, around Christmas time when the line-up was announced, rumours would go out that Blur were getting back together to do Glastonbury. Of course I knew it wasn't true, but it never stopped my heart leaping. I couldn't control how I felt. Nothing ever came of it and with every passing year it seemed less and less likely it would ever happen again. We were all drifting further and further apart.

I played the guitar every day, sang songs to the children. It was what I did with them, sang with them. The eldest asked me to come to his playgroup and sing some songs on the last Friday before Christmas.

It wasn't Glastonbury, but it was a gig. It was a pretty big day at playschool, too, the last one of the year and there was going to be a party with Father Christmas and presents.

It was bone-shakingly cold, when I arrived on the other side of the hill at the village hall, but it was toasty warm and cuddly inside. There was an enormous pot of tea and lots of tiny cups for the grown-ups. I was cosy, inside and out. My little boy ran around shouting, 'My daddy came! My daddy!'

First we said goodbye to all the children who were off to big school next term. They were all standing at the front in a neat little row, bewildered but very well behaved. Then we were on: me and my boy.

We kicked off with 'Dig, dig, digging', that was his favourite song. He stood there with his eyes closed and sang every word along with me. He was even getting the tune a bit. Kids really nail melodies. The way they say words is more appealing than people who can actually pronounce things properly. It kind of makes you think about the word when a child says it. Nothing can carry a simple melody quite like a child's voice. It's about the most ear-catching sound there is. Everything about toddlers is musical, really. 'Dig, dig, digging' is quite obscure but it went very well. Next we tried 'Bob the Builder', and I was almost knocked over. All the kids and all the mums joined in right from the top. They all knew all the words to the second verse and everything. We did it again, straight away.

'What do you want to do next?' 'I fought lawnmower,' he said, straight away, so I sang 'I Fought the Law'. The mums joined in with the 'I fought the law, anna law won' bits as well. I was enjoying it as much as I'd ever enjoyed playing with the band, anywhere. It was going well. I wanted to do 'Chirpy cheep cheep' next but I struggled with it, started it in the wrong key. It all fell apart. One of the mums started singing 'We Wish You a Merry Christmas', and all the others joined in. Everyone was smiling.

We finished with 'Stop the Cavalry'. Everyone sang. The parents were probably enjoying it more than the kids by that time – they were losing interest. It was time to go but it had been a big success. Ten minutes of loveliness. I rather wanted my wife and my children to see me doing my old job in front of a hundred thousand people as the sun went down on the Summer Solstice. Glastonbury would have been great, but second on the bill to Father Christmas was probably a much more important gig.

My dad clanged away on the piano. Claire was doing well with Mrs Swann. I was still absorbed by music. The house was full of it.

Every Christmas I get a little bit better at 'Walking in a Winter Wonderland'. The first chord of that song is B flat 13. I'd had a number one in Japan before I knew what that means. I'm still not sure if anybody does, really. The more you look at and know about B flat 13, the more impossible and unlikely it seems. Taken literally, it seems to be all the notes in the scale played at once: it seemed the height of sophistication and complexity, but clanging all the notes at once was exactly the way that the children attacked the piano.

For the first time since we signed to them, I didn't get a Christmas present from EMI. It wasn't because my musical output consisted only of nursery rhymes and mangled Christmassy jazz chords. The music business was changing. The company had been criticised for wasting money, hundreds of thousands of pounds on ridiculous expenses, including Christmas presents for its artists.

I always particularly looked forward to EMI's present. They were consistently well chosen. My favourite one ever was a candlestick that made cherubs go round in a circle ringing bells. I wondered if Queen all still had theirs, and Paul McCartney had his. I've still got my one. There must have been a board meeting and someone must have said, 'This has got to stop. It's ridiculous.' That was what was good about the music business, though. Making records is ridiculous, really. It can only be done by ridiculous people, and in a ridiculous manner. Farming was so straightlaced by comparison. Some of the local farmers came over as such serious no messing around types. No one needs to take anything that seriously. Anyway, round here they'd clearly been seriously struggling even to plant trees in the right place for the last couple of generations.

For our first Christmases here, when we were in search of a tree, Paddy sent us along to a vast estate he looked after locally, a castle in the middle of ten square miles of walled fields and forests near Stow-on-the-Wold. I called the head forester who said that we could come and choose a

Christmas tree. I knew lots of big estates grew them as a cash crop but I didn't know you could pick your own. Interestingly the biggest estates can be the hardest to find. Even with a GPS they can be tricky – the larger ones have up to three postcodes. They never have a house number, and the posher they are, the further they are from main roads. Even when you've found one of the gates, navigating around the inside is the difficult bit. Ten square miles. We went the wrong way several times with all the usual arguments and bother, but suddenly we were standing in a perfect spot surrounded by Christmas trees in the dusk. There was a lot of rustling and a bit of hooting and the odd scurry. Christmas trees have a happy life.

The forester was an authority on Christmas trees. There are many varieties and they had practically all of them on the estate. Those blue trees that don't drop the needles. They weren't so popular these days, he said. Someone he knew had planted hundreds of acres when they were at the peak of their popularity, and now they were ready to crop he couldn't sell them because people were going back to the traditional Norway Spruce. 'Picea Abies,' he said, wisely. They don't drop their needles anyway – not if you stand them in water.

What a fiendishly tricky business being a farmer is. It's not just being able to grow stuff, in the right place: that's the easy bit. You've got to be able to tell what people are going to want in future. Not just with trees, with anything. The market is always different when you're planting, from when you're selling. The most profitable farm business I'd heard of so far was one of the local farmers' wives'. She kept a pair of reindeer. They made good pets and fetched seven hundred quid an appearance at shopping centres at Christmas time. They were fully booked. That's got to be more than celebrities get paid for doing pantomime.

He was still happily telling us about his trees. There was a lot to know. The top bit where you put the fairy, from there down to the first set of buds, that's one year's growth. He had all sizes, neat little garden grids of trees of specific lengths. Mesmerising. We chose a three-storey whopper and he came round the next day with the thing lashed to his low loader. He'd even brought bits of rope for tying it off the banisters. I have always been a knot man, but his tying skills were in a different league, special Christmas tree knots I hadn't seen before that flew the thing plumb perpendicular right up the middle of the house. It just fitted inside the staircase and the top was an inch from the ceiling in the attic. It was big enough to climb. Not bad for fifty quid.

Trees belong to the class of things that cost as much money as you're prepared to spend, like pianos. If you're patient, you can always get a piano for nothing, especially grand pianos. Grand pianos are the best deal of all. They are more or less free to a good home. You can buy an upright that will stay in tune perfectly well for a hundred quid or so. If you want one that will tune to concert pitch, so you can play along to your favourite records, it'll cost about a thousand, and it keeps going up from there, way up. You can pay as much for a piano as for a house if you like. There were specimen trees in parkland of some of the big houses that were worth so much money they had to have their own security. Trees are such a huge part of life in the country. I marvelled at them all, from the thousand-year-old oaks at the bottom of our valley to the neat new rows of spruces at that estate.

The spruces seemed like a fantastically good deal. Such a good deal, I never planted any Christmas trees. There didn't seem any point. You could get lost and die of starvation in the Christmas tree forests on that estate. Miles and miles of them, a whole other world of pristine green symmetry that I assumed would keep us in Christmas trees forever, but it actually *was* rather too good to be true. The Christmas tree man was suddenly in all kinds of trouble with the authorities and his employer. I did always pay him cash, come to think of it.

Claire was so proud of having a big tree and so were the kids. We'd started with a whopper and nothing else would do now. I went out after another big one. Although you'd be hard pushed to find a square mile of the English countryside that doesn't harbour an overgrown Christmas tree plantation, I couldn't find anyone selling trees beyond eight feet tall. If you approach a man who is selling Christmas trees and tell him you want a really big one he rolls his eyes and gets out a calculator like you just asked him for something ridiculous, something almost impossible to engineer, something utterly absurd. It actually only takes about twelve years for a spruce to grow to fifteen feet, and they will all do it, too, if left completely undisturbed – it takes eight years to grow an ordinary one. Fortunately as was often the case in the parish, something that money apparently couldn't buy was available from a friend for nothing. Paddy said we could come and choose one from his father-in-law's belt and he'd chop it down and bring it over on the horsebox. The children were beside themselves, crying 'timber' as it fell. It filled the house with wonderful smells, resinous, sweet, floral, festive, 'Christmas on a stick'.

We didn't go out very much. In London people always wanted to meet in bars, restaurants or clubs. I rarely saw anyone's house unless it was three o'clock in the morning and everywhere had closed, but in the country people entertained mainly at home. When I was buying Christmas presents I noticed I was buying them all for people who lived in the neighbourhood, so we thought we'd have a Christmas party. My friend Robert came from America. I was really excited. When he arrived it was so cold in the house that I tried lighting a fire, but smoke just kept blowing back down the rotten chimney, setting off the fire alarms. That fireplace: whenever the wind blew from the north, the really cold wind, it just didn't work. I cursed the architect, the builders and my own stupidity, as I rubbed the heat on my hands into my trousers, having run outside several times, a sparking, smoking log in each hand. The wind was really howling and it was raining sideways. The fat logs continued burning, lying on the grass, drinking the breeze, sending sparking embers flying around the back garden.

That chimney is one of those things I'm always about to sort out. I had begun to make headway with it in fact, but it was one of the more tedious items on the long list of things that needed fixing. I had endless piles of lists of old stuff breaking, and new stuff not working properly. A fireplace that smoked when the wind was from due north didn't often make the top forty priorities. The heating in the smoked-out main room was broken as well and, come to think of it, so were half the lights. It was particularly cold in there, the heart of my house: my bleak, complicated mess of a house. Bill came over too. I found it quite awkward, being with an old friend and a new friend; probably the two people who I knew best but didn't know each other at all. Instead of being twice as nice as I'd hoped it would be, their presences were cancelling each other out a little bit. Perhaps really close friends don't mix. Intimacy doesn't work in parallel. There was nothing we could do to make it warmer, or less of an ill-lit mess, so we gave up and sat in another room, by a fire that did work. Bill started playing some old songs on the guitar he'd brought with him and gradually, with the music, the fussiness of the twenty-first century fell away and we were warm again, warm in a draughty cold old farmhouse, smiling and pulling silly faces as we sang.

The wind changed direction the next day and a fire was soon roaring in the grate, blazing away the cold and the last remnants of the black fug. There were about thirty people coming. I thought we'd cook one of our lambs. Everybody wanted to get involved. Some helped to build a bonfire in the garden, some were shoving carrots and garlic into the lamb, which Robert had washed in whisky and cut into four pieces. Everyone enjoyed lending a hand. It was so much better than nibbling peanuts and making small talk. I can't imagine anything that would have brought the early arrivals together more perfectly than helping to cook. Soon the house was buzzing, fires were roaring everywhere. Someone said it was the best lamb they'd ever tasted and everyone else agreed.

Christmas is absolutely my favourite time of year and it always has been. People would say things like, 'Don't you miss being in a band? You must miss it, though? I mean, don't you miss the adulation? The attention? Surely you must miss all that? It must be tough for you, missing it like you must miss it?' For sure, being in the band was fab, but as time wore on I wondered if it was just being young and free from responsibility that I missed the most, just being able to grab my passport and go to New York at the drop of a hat. Even in the good old days, I seem to remember missing the old days. I think no matter what you do or how successful you are, nothing in life can ever be anywhere near as much fun as being young at Christmas time. Those are the times I like to recall: childhood

Christmases. And now I was relishing the thought of reliving it with my own children, even if the senior members of the family had abandoned us. All of a sudden we had five children.

By the time we had three children, we rarely got invited anywhere. With four children, no one even wanted to come and see us. When we hit five, even the grandparents chose to avoid us over Christmas. It was only the second time I hadn't spent it with them – I slept through 1994 and missed everything completely. Claire's folks, too, were a little apprehensive about coming now we had so many kids, so it was just us.

The songs have pretty much stayed the same but, my, oh my, the food has changed. My grandad was a chef. He was always up to something with breadcrumbs or brine, particularly at Christmas. The essence of Christmas itself is his stuffing recipe. Every time I see or smell stuffing, I am transported back to his kitchen. There were all kinds of seasonal, local organic delights on offer at Daylesford, but I'm a sucker for what I grew up with. Christmas was time for Corona Cream Soda, sticks of celery painted with tube cheese and Babycham. My sister and I always got quarter bottles in our stockings every year. I reintroduced the tradition. I still like Babycham but the tiny bottle-shaped chocolate liqueurs are the best thing about Christmas. The newsagents in Chippy, the nearest town, was run entirely by elderly persons and children, and always had a fantastic selection of fireworks and chocolate liqueurs. It harked back to another era.

In the seventies the more packaged up and processed something was, the further it had come, the more we wanted it. The more that had happened to it, the better. If it was frozen, vac-packed, dehydrated, tinned or brightly coloured, you knew you could trust it. Angel Delight is nearly all of those things, and it has to be said, much nicer than rhubarb. There were still only three crisp flavours when I was young and everything was a lot smaller, apart from Wagon Wheels, which were as big as pizzas, but only because pizzas then were tiny, and always frozen. When my grandad died, we went to live in the big house he ran as a hotel in the summer, so I grew up with a proper commercial kitchen, an enormous larder, whizzer machines, cleavers, the works, which was quite fortunate because having five children is like running a bed and breakfast. It's like doing Christmas every day.

I went for a drink at the pub in the village on Christmas Eve. Someone was talking on a mobile. 'I'm stuck in the middle of nowhere,' he said. He was in a panic, trying to escape. There was nowhere I wanted to be more. One man's middle of nowhere is the centre of another man's universe. By the end of lunchtime it seemed very still and quiet as if the whole place were just about to set like a jelly. Right across the valley, apart from the odd sheep coughing, birds were making the only sounds. It was grey and damp and beautiful. A home is never more of a home than when it's wet and windy, dark and dirty out and Christmas. The house looked so pretty during the long nights, warm light glowing in the windows. Gaslight was probably even prettier, and candles prettier still. The past was beautifully lit. New light bulbs are so lab-like, clinical. We were seeing the last of the tungsten Christmases.

It was warm in the village church. I shuddered to think of the heating bill and wondered who was going to pay it. As I settled into the bus lane 'oi oi oi, oggi oggi oggi' of the service, so far out of kilter with the whizz-bangs of the twenty-first century, I couldn't ever recall being warm in a church before, even in summer. The stillness of churches is supreme at Christmas, a balm to calm the mad fizz, and I dissolved peacefully into the benevolence. The Midnight Carol Service had been moved forward an hour, a misplaced nod to popular demand. Some people in the village had been complaining that midnight was just too late. I went with Claire and three generations of our neighbour's family. The adjusted timing meant skipping coffee in order to get there in time for 'Hark the Herald Angels'. I was belting out the tune without a care in the world and quite a big grin on my face already, when quite unexpectedly the girls in the row behind us started to sing the descant harmonies as the first chorus kicked in.

It was the most surprising sensation, as if our singing was being caressed. I looked around and they were all smiling as they sang those exquisite wavering high notes. It was like taking off, becoming completely weightless, leaving the world behind altogether. I closed my eyes and fell into their voices. Singing in harmony at Christmas time. It was bliss.

We turned and spoke to them in excited whispers at the end of the song. 'That was incredible,' we all gushed, and invited them to come home with us. I worked out what I reckoned our share of the heating was and threw it into the collection plate during 'Come All Ye Faithful'. Losing myself in those ancient tunes, songs I've known and loved since childhood, some of them hundreds of years old. I never thought I'd enjoy church more than opening presents but that was almost heaven.

High noon of Christmas is just after the turkey plates have been cleared and before the cheese comes out. It's a perfect moment, that Christmas Day cheese pause. It's what we all work towards. It's plain sailing after the cheese comes out.

We walked to the big oak with a long piece of rope and made a swing before collapsing in front of the fire. One of the neighbours brought a muntjac deer over in the evening: my favourite thing to eat. You can't buy them. He'd shot it himself on Christmas morning. It was all I wanted for Christmas. So much had changed in my life. I managed to spend all of Boxing Day in my pyjamas, but got dressed the following day to go for a walk with a metal detector I had been given. I didn't find any buried treasure but I hadn't had cause to have a really thorough poke around in that bit of woodland before, and it slowly became apparent that the whole copse was an ancient overgrown formal garden. Still no sign of the missing cricket pitch, though.

My shoes went missing for a few days and it didn't really seem to matter. We did the rounds of the houses. It was more than five years since Blur had made a record. I had another life now. Ironically, Claire had become something similar to a rock star kind of person. Everyone talked about her. We went to the big house on top of the hill for drinks. They had had builders for ten years. I was pouring myself some tea in the kitchen, discussing the football match that had just taken place in the garden. I was talking to a willowy lady, a grand dame with the brightest eyes. I said my name was Alex, and she said 'Oh, you're the one who—' at this point people usually said 'who used to be in that band', but she said, 'Oh, you're the one whose wife has had five children.'

The future always looks so uncluttered, full of more space and time than it actually is. I imagined there would be time to do jigsaws, think about the year ahead, doing very little for once, but doing next to nothing is absolutely impossible at Christmas with a young family. It's the busiest time of year. Claire spent a lot of time on the phone organising a New Year's Eve party at our neighbours' house, which grew explosively from a sit down dinner to a wedding-style extravaganza with a marquee, DJ and karaoke box. It was an excellent party. I sang myself hoarse trying to reach the high notes in 'Livin' on a Prayer', danced myself stupid with teenagers and found a huge cheeseboard just when I was starting to flag. We got home about five and quite a lot of people came too. Someone started playing the piano and I set up the drumkit in the hall. That was a good decision. It sounded great in there. It woke the chickens up, but not the children. New Year's Day found the house in the hands of the children, as we cowered under the duvet. As adults we choose to start the year in pieces. It's definitely the right way to do it, from one's bed. Children get whatever they want on New Year's Day. It's probably better than Christmas Day if you're under ten.

I'd picked up quite a lot of bad habits from being in a band but the only one that I really struggled to lose was smoking. I smoked all the time. I didn't know how many, daren't count, so many that every time I got a sore throat I was convinced I had cancer and every cough was almost certainly early-onset emphysema. I had to stop. I was someone's father.

My whole life had been a non-stop binge of self-indulgence. I had responsibilities now. I had to give up smoking. I stopped smoking and started running. And how fine it was to take the air after a marathon session of half awake sloth by the fireside. The sun broke through the silver morning sky and it was as if I'd never eaten all those Quality Street. A huge roe deer broke cover from the woods and passed within yards of me: utterly enchanting. It was as grey as battleships up above and beautifully soft underfoot, cool and inviting. I smoked my last cigarette, took to my heels and ran off over the fields. I hadn't done that for years. I ran and ran, kept going, until after an hour or so I had no idea where I was, in the middle of a big wood, puffing gently. I hadn't seen a soul since I set out and had settled into a rhythmic trance.

It was very Christmassy in the hedgerows: hips and holly. I suppose it had something to do with the euphoria of a fast beating heart, of the primal pleasure of running into nowhere as fast as I could, but away from one-dimensional high street chains and brands that change hands is a constant and far more beautiful place. Those hedges looked more lovely than I remembered – they always do.

CHAPTER 5

HOT SHOTS

There were so many beautiful women in the Cotswolds, some lived in castles and some lived in caravans. There were dowager châtelaines who presided over great swathes of countryside, heiresses who married into royalty. There were marchionesses with hounds, and ladies on horseback. London was such a masculine environment. By comparison the countryside seemed to be in the hands of women; strong-willed and beautiful women who were used to getting exactly what they wanted. They ran the households and the social occasions. Men could only rise so far up the social ladder.

Lately even pubs were full of ladies having lunch instead of men getting drunk.

* * *

Everyone said the rooks were a nuisance and the eight-acre wood was full of them. People said the rooks eat all the other birds' eggs, and that they made a right mess. Fred told me they pecked out newborn lambs' eyes. Anyone and everyone who saw them flocking in clouds at the northern end of the eight-acre wood said we'd have to do something about them. So I had to get a gun. If you need a gun, these days, it's quite complicated. A shotgun licence is the most straightforward. Rifles are a bit more tricky. Pistols are very complicated, and almost no one has cannons any more. Anyone who wants to secure a weapons licence, of whatever level, needs a weapons safe and a 'suitable reason', which come to think of it can only ever really be 'because I want to shoot stuff'. I sent off about twenty photos to the police station and made an appointment. I'd been a bit apprehensive about the firearms officer's visit. Someone told me that two of them come around and shine lights in your face and try to make you 'crack'. It was just one guy on his own, though, nice bloke. 'I was a vegetarian for ages,' I told him, 'but then we bought this farm.'

He agreed that I needed a gun for vermin control. It was true, of course. It was obvious. But when it came to it, I was quite surprised that was all it took.

He said I'd probably need a rifle for the rats, eventually, and he drew a picture of a rifle bullet. It was a small bullet. He said I'd probably need a rifle that fired a bullet about that big, to begin with. Then he drew another bullet, which was a bit bigger and said we'd need one that big if we wanted to shoot the deer but the trouble was they could kill a person two miles away. It was about an inch long.

He said if we were having problems with deer, and they can be a nuisance, it was either shooting them or reintroducing bears. He did go on to talk about an elephant gun he'd seen at Holland & Holland that fired huge missiles, but I had the idea. Guns are a kind of spanner and you need the right size spanner.

I got a shotgun which fires a spray of pellets and a couple of kittens to take care of the rats.

After years of razzle-dazzle I came to enjoy simple pleasures. I liked walking. I liked sitting by the fire. I liked cooking. These are all good things. I remember hearing Paul McCartney explain how he stopped eating meat when he moved to a farm. Exactly the opposite thing happened to me. I had been a vegetarian for almost twenty years when we arrived.

It was clear to me from watching Fred's sheep that it was all fine being a sheep while it lasted. I'm not sure if the same is true for most chickens, but sheep don't have it too bad at all. To have been a lamb and then be roast, is better than never to have been a lamb at all, I began to think, and it wasn't long before I was tucking in.

I had to call for help with the rooks, but I had a triumph with the dishwasher. It was with a sinking heart that I discovered the stupid thing wasn't emptying properly, but sometimes a man's got to do what a man's got to do, like it or not. I managed to fix it single-handed. If I'd been a forest-dwelling hunter-gatherer and I'd slain a rabid rampaging wolf with my bare hands, I couldn't have been more cock-a-hoop with chest-beating male pride. The part of a man that mends dishwashers is exactly the same part that kills monsters. I was always reluctant to rise to the role of monster conqueror.

There were always people passing through the farm doing this, that, and the other. A number of passers-through had pointed out that among my newly acquired chickens, there were four cockerels. Two or three people had shaken their heads at the birds and muttered words to the effect of 'You know what you've got to do.' It didn't look like I would need to do anything. For a good while there'd been nothing to worry about. They pecked around contentedly like Showaddywaddy, all matching suits and thrusting, lifting my spirits, cock-a-doodling their joy and egging for England. Those hens were a PR machine for country living. Nothing made visitors happier than half a dozen eggs. There was a point when it seemed eggs were a more appropriate thing to send people on their way with than Blur's greatest hits.

Maybe it was because they finally reached a certain age, but as predicted, two of the cocks suddenly started fighting.

It was a horrible thing to watch: every time I went to see them they were relentlessly, viciously stabbing at each other in a constant kerfuffle, both their necks blood spattered. It was horrendous. The time to act had come.

I asked my neighbour to the north, a devout Christian, to give me a hand. He'd grown up with chickens and he knew the drill. Cocks will fight until there is only one standing so it really is best to step in and make things as painless as possible.

Some people suggested shooting them in the head with air pistols, some said blast them with shotguns, but the most humane way is to break their necks.

First we had to catch the cockerels, which isn't easy. By the time I was holding on to one my heart was already beating fast. You take the legs in your left hand and the head in the other. Then you pull the neck firmly over your right thigh until it clicks. It took all my strength. The wings flap a lot after the bird is dead, which adds to the over the top melodrama of the situation, and by the time we'd dispatched all three surplus birds my pulse was racing hard from physical exertion and the awful glamour of death. Peace was restored in the chicken run.

It was a bread and butter January day, and everyone was head-down, arse-up, pedalling hard: even the children. Even in the woods, the animals seemed busy, gangs of skinny deer dashing about with great purpose like teenagers on a Saturday night. Ah, to be a part of all that whirring industry under comforting grey skies. I found it far more compelling than Manhattan during Fashion Week.

It was cold, though, and when it's cold it's really cold.

There was a rumour that Chippy, the town, was the coldest in England. It is hundreds of feet above sea level. East of the hills at the southern end of the valley, there is no higher ground as far as Russia and the wind lashed in across the whole length of Europe. Heating bills at the grander addresses – the abbeys, priories and prebendal houses, not to mention the stately homes – ran to tens, even hundreds of thousands of pounds.

Until very recently, logs, hot water bottles and woolly jumpers were the only thing that kept people warm out here in winter. I spent weeks absorbed with reclaimed, polished cast-iron radiators, with thermostatic valves and super-efficient wet underfloor heating with complicated manifolds and neat little switches, twin timers, dual cylinders and parallel boilers. It was all so complicated and nothing worked as well as the fireplaces that had been there for a hundred years. They all worked brilliantly. Fires are a great system. You can burn wood that you've grown yourself for as long as you like.

I now know we'll never manage to get through a whole winter here without some kind of heating headache. Cars hardly ever go wrong any more, but heating has got more and more complicated. So sophisticated it is always breaking down. I'd already called the plumber about the underfloor heating and the Aga man, as both had conked out, when the entire system went down. I thought that completely rebuilding the house would take care of those kinds of problems but that's the great con of grand designs, there is no such thing as a house where everything works. Having everything working is only something that can be approached, not actually achieved. There is always one more thing that needs doing – no such thing as no problems, only different problems. You take away the problem of being cold but you replace it with the problems of heating systems. Maybe we overrate the idea of being warm anyway. The kids didn't notice the heating wasn't working. None of them even wanted to put their dressing gowns on, or their slippers, but I had to tell the ladies of the house, who were all suffering, that if they were really cold, to go outside for a couple of minutes, then come back in again. That way it suddenly felt much warmer inside.

We'd had a fair few cold snaps, but the heating went just when it got really bitter. Everything else stopped working as well. Even the external doors – things with just one moving part – seemed to be struggling with seasonal adjustment disorders. Every single door needed some kind of attention. Most of them were jamming shut. There was a danger we'd be stuck inside until spring.

Then suddenly it was like we were living in a cartoon. We'd woken up somewhere else without going anywhere: the familiar landscape recast in angelica, in candied green and stretching forever into perfect blue. The blissful silence and timelessness of a minus-ten frost. It was perfectly clear and things in the distance, villages that are miles away, seemed close enough to reach out and touch. I've seen perspective completely broken like that in Greenland before, but it was unexpected in Oxfordshire.

The air we were breathing had been supplied directly from Russia and was so fresh you could taste it on every breath. The children licked their lips while stomping icy puddles. I fiddled with a huge bonfire that was set in the yard. Soon an inferno was blazing and all the debris that was cluttering the house and the barnyard went on it and we warmed ourselves on the blaze between stamping puddles. Once we'd shattered every one we walked down to the pond sucking icicles. It was hard to believe there could be an engine powerful enough to freeze the whole thing overnight but sure enough it looked solid enough to walk on. The dog went skittering across. Some cheered him on, and some shouted at him to come off. I wondered if I would be able to run over the ice to the island in the middle. I put one foot on the ice to test it. There was a big crack as I fell flat on my back. I lay there trying not to break the ice. I just about managed to wriggle back without going under. Dangerous, that stuff.

Just when it seemed like it couldn't get any prettier, it started to snow, gentle flakes falling in still cool air. Hot tea tasted better than vintage champagne.

I must have run a hundred and fifty miles that week, all over the valley in perfect solitude: bliss – and then, misery. I grated a shin and blackened a toenail on the home straight, tripped over a branch and wiped out completely in the eight-acre wood. I can't tell you how frustrating that was. I actually screamed, not in pain, but annoyance. As I tumbled onto my face it struck me that this was easily the messiest woodland in the whole valley. All the neighbouring woods had belonged to the same families for generations and they knew how to look after them. I'd had a forester in there the previous autumn, but he'd only done half the job. He'd cut down all the weakest trees but he still hadn't removed any of the brash from the tracks.

Still, there's no better way of keeping abreast of everything that's going on and what needs taking care of, than padding around the place. I'd become completely familiar with the landscape and felt a part of it.

I spent a fortune on heating that didn't work, trying to get the best. As an afterthought I'd also bunged a budget sauna heater in one of the old sheds. I think it's probably the best two hundred quid I've ever spent, that heater. I sat in there, perspiration teeming, watching the snow waft down in flakes on the other side of the window. The snow was deep, deep enough to dive underneath, which I did, in my pants, screaming. The well in the back garden definitely had potential as a plunge pool, too.

All the big farm machinery was scrambled to take care of the animals but it was hard to say whether the sheep had noticed anything different was happening, really. Perhaps they were all chewing a bit faster, like Alex Ferguson in injury time.

There was about two feet of snow. In London, usually ninety minutes away, life was going on as normal. Out here, entire communities were cut off. Roads were completely impassable and the world fell into immaculate silence. It was hard to grasp how, even in the twenty-first century, great swathes of the countryside could be completely disconnected from the rest of the world by such a simple thing as a good covering of snow.

I loved it. The quad bike came into its own at last. Claire took it to Daylesford to get food. It had become easy to spend all day thinking about food, as I became more and more absorbed by the farm and the vegetable garden but now it was all hidden by snow and out of reach.

In the first few months we lived here, I'd received letters from various people asking if they could come and shoot on the land. I'd never given it much thought but once I'd realised I'd have to get a gun myself, and especially now they were thrown into relief by the snow, I started to eye up the game birds that were straying onto my patch. It's delicious, pheasant, roasted with bread sauce.

Most of the big estates round and about still bred pheasants and a day's shooting was like the countryside equivalent of the Oscars: the ultimate ticket.

I received an extravagantly embossed card from the nearest castle inviting me to join them on a driven shoot. Strictly speaking, I discovered, it wasn't called a castle. It was an abbey, surrounded on all sides as far as the eye could see by immaculate formal gardens under the weight of the winter sky, parkland stretching in all directions.

A driven shoot is about the most expensive way of wasting time anyone has ever dreamed up. It requires vast swathes of immaculately maintained countryside and a whopping cast: beaters, keepers, loaders and dog handlers.

Then there's all the gear involved; togs, guns, sticks, bags and cartridges: endless. I learned very quickly that no matter how spectacular the house or how magnificent the landscape, shooting is only ever as much fun as the other people who will be there. These can range from bores and bullies to royals and celebrities. About half the party is guaranteed to be sickeningly rich and slightly bored of everything.

Some of my neighbours were completely addicted to shooting. There was one guy who lived in the nicest house I've ever seen. I sometimes came home a different way, just to catch a glimpse of that house. I was pleased to meet him and gushed and expounded at length about how beautiful his house was. As time went on whenever I went on a local shoot he'd be there and we'd be introduced again and I'd say 'We've met before, I used to be in a band,' and I could see he'd have absolutely no recollection of who I was. He had no idea who the band were, or anything. As far as I could tell he'd spent his whole life moving from castle to abbey shooting stuff with other people, many of them just like he was. His riches had cut him off from the world and suffocated him in the same way that poverty might.

I could only face a big shoot about twice a year. It's a whole day. Plus you often have to go for dinner the night before. It was good to see those big old country houses firing on all cylinders. I'd bring my gun and my guitar and we'd all be up singing until the small hours, singing all the songs I could remember. There'd always be sore heads at the breakfast table but the atmosphere was jocular, festive.

Usually most of the party would have known each other since they were at school and the estates that ran shoots always boasted very well staffed, well-run houses. Cooks in the kitchen and boys in the bootroom, porridge and papers, coffee and cigarettes: an English breakfast banquet. Fires roared and elegant young men buttled around the banter soothing and assuaging, dodging jokes, delivering eggs.

The first time I went, I was apprehensive. It was quite a famous shoot. One of the party was said to be the best shot in England. The pheasants were legendary, too. Fast, high, curling birds. Pheasants fly the fastest of all the game species and there was quite a good chance I wouldn't hit anything all day long. Then there's always the chance of getting shot, or shooting someone. I wondered what would be worse over my third cup of coffee. Guns make me nervous. The châtelaine had recently taken a pellet in the face, and her best hat had been ruined. She was still upset about that hat.

Down tracks and alongside streams we bumped and skidded: loaders, goaders, pickers-up and eight tweedy guns in a cavalcade of 4x4s, dogs of all sizes in the back, arriving in a remote and silent valley, a flat grassy riverbed with woodland rising up on either side in smudges of mist. It was still early, still drizzling, but not cold. We adjusted to our surroundings, falling quiet and motionless, drinking in the landscape, listening to the faint sounds of nowhere, slowly becoming part of it all. It was beautiful, far from the present, from telephones, computers, families and work. I forgot everything as we waited quietly for the birds to rise. The beaters approached through the trees. I heard dogs, whistles, the odd shout and clap. Nothing, nothing, nothing and then all hell broke loose: bang, bang, kerbang as a cloud of partridge rose first. It was heart-stopping, particularly for the birds. The partridge were racing directly towards the line of guns and were followed by wave upon wave of pheasants rushing overhead. Hundreds and hundreds of birds. Dogs dashing, guns blazing – guns that cost more than a house – insults flying like bullets, birds flailing and falling. Total exhilaration.

By the time we stopped for soup and sherry, I'd hit half a dozen birds, better than I thought I'd manage all day. It felt like Christmas morning. One of the keepers had managed to tickle a trout from the stream between drives, and it sat alongside the crates of birds in the back of the gamekeeper's jeep. The sun was just reaching over the tree-tops on the far side of the valley, warming us in gold light. There is no finer way to get lunch.

Shooting has become more popular over the past decade and it was a big industry to start with. It takes a huge amount of resources to raise and shoot a pheasant: acres and acres of well-maintained Grade I English countryside, a fully-staffed castle, a vast team of gamekeepers, beaters, loaders, dog trainers, dog handlers and shooters.

Partridge is absolutely delicious too. They're just small delicious chickens. Chickens live in cages and taste a bit like chicken. Game birds taste a bit like chicken and live on fantastic, historic country estates.

It struck me in the butcher's, as I looked at the neat rows of game birds, that they had all probably been shot by company directors, CEOs, billionaires and spare members of the royal family – all taking the day off work and paying a huge amount for the privilege. Not a bad way to go. Whenever I see game for sale, I grab it. It's about the best bargain going. It's hard to think of how an animal could be more ethically reared, or how it could be made any more expensive.

I wasn't very comfortable with the idea of making sport out of killing things, I hadn't been a vegetarian for twenty years for no reason, but there's something holistic about bagging your dinner with a shotgun. Buying organic, ethical, biodynamic, rare breed meat was definitely a step in the right direction, but if you eat meat, at some point, something has to die and who better to pull the trigger than the person who's going to eat the thing?

Funnily enough the rooks, the reason why I'd got the gun in the first place, didn't need shooting at all. Despite what everyone had told me, they don't cause much harm and it's best to leave them be.

All the farmers, including myself, put food down for the game birds to encourage them onto our patches away from their breeding grounds. It's called 'feeding in'. I put a barrel of grain into each of the three woods to see what would happen. There was usually about one bird in each small wood, and two in the big one.

I wandered about the farm with the dog, picked off a handful of stray pheasant and hung them up in one of the barns. Pheasants are pretty birds.

The shooting isn't actually the nasty bit. It's exactly the same feeling as lining up a long red on a snooker table. Plucking is where it starts to get horrible. I haven't had much experience with these things, very few people have I suppose, but by the time the last one was dangling, I was toughened-up.

I thought I'd dress the birds myself, just to see how it was done. Paddy came to lend a hand. It takes ages. Absolutely ages. You start at the base of a wing, pulling little clumps of feathers off. Pretty soon you're up to your knees in feathers, and the bird still looks much the same as it did when you started. If you become impatient and start ripping off big handfuls, the skin starts to tear, and then you're in all kinds of trouble. I couldn't believe how bad my bird smelled. 'Wow, they really smell, don't they?' I said. Paddy told me I'd soon get used to it but it seemed to get worse.

Paddy was quick. He'd done three in the time it took me to do one but eventually we were both ready for the next phase: the chopping block and the cleaver. It was an ever more gruesome story. They were already pretty mangled. First you chop off the head, wings and feet, and then you're getting close to something that's starting to look what you might see cling-wrapped in a supermarket. You still need to get the guts out though. That's a really nasty business, the worst bit. You make a cut in the base of the ribcage and plunge a couple of fingers right inside. All the neat little intestines come out in a plug, but you have to really rummage around in there to pluck the heart out. It's all spikey inside. There is something very scary about anyone who can take the guts out of a bird whilst keeping a straight face. Paddy couldn't manage it either. There was a lot of eye rolling and lip curling.

I brought my nearly bald bird to the butcher block and he said 'Jesus! What is that smell?' I said 'That's what I'm talking about, maybe I've hung them for too long.' It was only mine that smelled like that, though. It must have been lying around decomposing for a couple of weeks already when the dog had picked it up. On some driven shoots the keepers pluck the birds during lunch and vacuum pack them with bacon on their backs for you to take home. The butcher up the road did a good line in plucking and drawing game birds for one pound fifty a head. Having spent the afternoon wrestling with a stinking corpse, I thought that was good value.

I loved the freezing, dark winter months in the countryside. They're underrated. March and April can mope on forever if it's cold and wet, but in the deep midwinter, nothing is as cosy as a roaring fire, a houseful of people and a fully extended table groaning with food. I grew to love dinner parties.

No one ever said 'We're having a dinner party,' any more. The words had become unmentionable, but dinners soon became the entire basis of my social life. I liked cooking them and going to them. In fact I liked everything about them. The gentle formality, the serenity and comfort of an evening spent in someone's home with good food. London has some of the world's best restaurants, but I'd rather go to someone's house for dinner, than eat in any of them. The bigger houses often had chefs. There's only one thing nicer than having someone to cook for you and that's knowing how to cook. I love messing around with food and cooked everything from whole pigs on bonfires to petits fours in portable ovens.

There was always a lot going on if you knew where to look. A tiny hand-written sign at the farm next door read 'Hound Racing' and up the little track a tall, thin man was doing his best to get the ins and outs of it across: 'The idea is that you bid. You bid to buy the dog. You will then own that dog. You will own that dog purely for the duration of the race. If your dog wins, you take half the pot. Do you understand?' We understood. He was clearly a pleasant fellow, addressing a tight puddle of tweed through a megaphone. It was all very jolly. I knew it would be. There had been much excitement about it in the big houses. There was a makeshift track maybe two hundred yards long, half a dozen jumps constructed from hay bales and the hounds of the local hunt.

The kids had their heart set on buying the dog with the black collar, but I pulled them out of the bidding at the fifty-quid level, losing out on the sale to a regal fourteen-year-old. There was a tote system in operation too, a picnic table manned by stable girls. We stuck a fiver on the black dog.

It was a well-attended occasion, without being busy: a rarefied version of a crowd, a kind of backstage feeling on a sunny breezy Sunday afternoon. I hadn't had much to do with the hunt since we arrived. I let them come over the land because the master of the hounds asked me nicely, but here they all were and suddenly there was nothing so delightful as being idle, dog trading with rich people.

The black dog won. The kids had won seven quid, but they thought they'd won the dog and were inconsolable.

The glow of the tail lights of Fred's Land Rover down by the sheep barn, drew me in that direction as I took the evening air. It wasn't cold and the moon was up. We'd been taking a battering all week and it was still soggy underfoot, but for the moment, clement. Fred was marching around purposefully in the dark. 'That scatty one's had it, Gor!' he said and nodded in the direction of the place where he left dead sheep for collection. Then he led me into the huge shed where the January ewes were lambing, a tatty old 'L'-shaped barn. One end was open, one wall made from wood, another out of breezeblock and the last, the one that makes the 'L'-shape, a down-and-out Duchess of a beautiful aged Cotswold stone wall, the recycled remnant of an earlier building. Despite being built purely along the lines of functionality without the slightest consideration of even the most basic aesthetic principles, the shed had a quality of magnificence about it. I guess you can always find the beauty in anything, but beauty definitely wasn't put here. It just arrived, unexpected when the thing was finished. The shed was actually built for cattle, so it was luxury length and king-size, and that tin pot palace radiated a church-like vastness and peace. Holiness was in there too that night, I suppose, if there was ever such a thing.

Despite its immensity, the place was cosy. The open end was barricaded with a makeshift wall of double height, one-tonne hay bales that made the Cotswold stone look lacklustre by comparison. The gold stuff was knee deep and snug wall to wall. Plumped on top and nestling and gambolling among it were a legion of fresh lambs and their mothers.

Most of the ewes have twins, but there are always quite a few triplets and there had also been two lots of quads. The ewes rarely need any help lambing. Fred needed to be on call just in case, but he did like being there and watching. When they come out they're all ready to go. They're up on the bounce straight away with a buoyancy that would melt the hardest heart. We were both smiling. Come to think of it, Fred's always smiling.

We were so lucky to inherit sheep when we moved in here. They smell nice. They look nice. They taste nice. Sheep farming is naturally quite an extensive, organic business. There is nothing horrible about any of it. The easiest way to do it is to let them run around outside in the summer and have them in the sheds lambing when it's cold and wet. There's no need to pump chemicals onto the fields to make the grass grow. It's all pretty wholesome and simple.

On the other hand, the arrangement between Fred and I had become quite complicated, we were buying and selling sheep to each other as I converted the farm to organic. It was difficult for him to change his ways. He thought the world had gone mad. He'd spent his life rearing sheep and winning prizes for it and now here I was, a blow-in know nothing, telling him he had to do it differently.

CHAPTER 6

CHEESE

February is a wonderful month, meteorologically speaking. It's a big time for prevailing conditions, and living in the country, conditions really prevail. Weather is the biggest difference between town and country. All meteorological conditions are a misery in the city and it's no wonder people are always moaning about the weather. You don't really get the whole picture, weather-wise, in built-up areas. You just get a slice. It's like not being able to see the telly when you can hear it. It's annoying. Out in the deep end of the countryside, there were horizons in all directions and a big sky. It all makes more sense in glorious technicolour and surround sound. The deep frosts were exquisite, often associated with clear skies, and pulling up the blinds in the morning on a bright frozen landscape with mist lingering here and there, is a jaw dropper. There is clarity in the atmosphere in the winter months that fades into a haze with the warmer weather. Haziness and warmth go hand in hand. The summer landscape is softer, with leaves on the trees and hedges, and fancier shapes. Midwinter is all about sharp corners and bright light. You can see for miles.

There wasn't much to do in the evenings in the country in February, but I certainly had my hands full, absorbed in the day-to-day minutiae of the farm. It was like running a small country with enough intrigue and drama to keep me occupied. There was a particularly tedious ongoing problem with the oil supply to the Aga so I spent a lot of time cooking on the little seventies electric stove that was already in the ramshackle kitchen when we arrived. It was soup season and I became a soup convert. There was something about the farmhouse kitchen that made me fearless. I played with my grandad's stock recipe. It was relaxing. Making stock involved just the right amount of effort for a winter's evening. Food always feels the most nourishing in midwinter.

February had always made me think of grey, drizzly, cold days. It is cold, usually, although some calm mornings as the whole thing sputtered into spring, it was warm enough for me to take my coffee in the sun outside in my pants. Then it would go back to midwinter, but a completely grey day, a Yarborough deal, is quite impossible. There were always black bits and silver streaks, and it tended to pour, rather than drizzle, in February. When the wind was howling and the rain was beating against the windows, I never thought about switching the television on. We spent more time watching the fire, than watching the telly. It makes staying in so much more appealing, when it's foul. It was nicer to have a reason to stay in, than a reason to go out, as I got older.

Paddy said, 'Do you like cheese?'

I told him I did. I did in fact, probably more than anybody else I'd ever met, like cheese and it hadn't gone unnoticed. Even in Japan, where there is no exact word for 'cheese', they tracked the stuff down, threw it at me on stage and presented it to me in hotel lobbies. I've had cheeses thrown at me in many countries, I said, but I recalled Japan because there it comes in tins. Aside from the immediate hazard of low-flying vacuum-packed Camembert, I always liked to keep an eye on the cheese situation at large when I was on the move and for many years saw touring with the band merely as an excuse to travel the world tracking down and eating obscure kinds of cheese. Cheese was on the rider. Cheese was *de rigueur*. Cheese was what I liked a lot. I said to Paddy, 'Yes I do like cheese. Why?'

Paddy said there was a cheesemaker returning to the village and he was looking for somewhere to make the stuff. I think I must have gone quite quiet. I remember the exact feeling when Blur won a Brit award for the first time, but this felt better than that. I'd never really wanted a Brit award. It was certainly a nice thing to have, but I'd never really yearned for one. My own cheese was something I must have wanted for as long as I could remember.

The cheesemaker was called Roger Crudge and he came over on his bicycle from Kingham. He had some cheese with him that he'd made and it was delicious. I'd had something similar on a Swiss mountain slope but not before or since. It was like a light coming on. I knew straight away, as soon as I tasted that cheese, that this was what I wanted to do. 'Let's build it. Let's build a factory,' I said, straight away. 'Let's just do it! I'm in. What's it going to take?' I'd been messing around, getting to grips with my little slice of England but now with one mouthful of cheese I had found a purpose. I knew what I was meant to be doing. It had been staring me in the face all along. How could it not have been easier to see? Claire actually liked cheese almost as much as I did, too. It's always so hard to know what to do until it's blindingly obvious.

We sat, Crudgie and I, and talked for a long time about cheese. I told him of my quest to track down the spookiest cheese in the world, the brown cheese of North Norway. They eat it there for breakfast. After years of searching I found it by accident taking a hungover chomp into a breakfast bun in a two-star hotel on a day off. The taste was so powerful that my eyes nearly popped out. I couldn't swallow it and had to drink lots of water. I was slightly ashamed that I still hadn't been able to pluck up the courage to return to it.

I liked all the other cheeses I'd ever tried, though, and I had so many questions all of a sudden. What sort of cheese was he going to make? Was it difficult?

'Of course it's not difficult,' he said. 'All kinds of cheese are made from the same ingredients and it is quite a simple process. I'll show you how to do it right now if you like.' I didn't know you even could make cheese, just like that. These days I thought you needed, well I had no idea what you needed, someone's permission? Of course it must have been made here on the farm for generations, but so had bacon and now you needed all kinds of paperwork to do that from scratch.

Roger said he would just need some milk and a lemon and while we were talking he warmed the milk and squirted the lemon into it.

All cheese, he said, has just four ingredients. Milk is the most important, so the first thing we would need to do would be to get a regular supply. Then we'd have to decide whether to pasteurise. We'd get consistent results from pasteurised milk and we'd be much less likely to kill anybody, but untreated milk makes better cheese. 'Milk,' he said, 'has a new vintage every day and when you start to standardise it, you lose the subtler flavours. And,' he explained carefully, 'you don't want to do that.'

It is true. Like plums on a plum tree, no two raw milk cheeses are ever exactly the same. He explained the one we'd just eaten would be illegal in America. 'It's quite safe to use untreated milk for cheese,' he said. 'Well, quite safe.'

I wondered where we'd get some dairy cows. Roger seemed to think that it would probably be too expensive and take too long to start a new dairy herd as well as a new cheese. He was all for keeping things as simple as possible so it'd be best to get the milk delivered in a tank, twice a week.

He said he wanted to start with cows' milk cheese similar to the one we'd just tasted but he wanted to 'play around' with sheep and goat milk too. Reindeer, camel and giraffe were all options, as well. He'd obviously spent a long time thinking about it, the way he reeled them off. Not all types of milk would work, though, it has to be the milk of a ruminant, a cud-chewing mammal because those are the only milks that will coagulate.

Cheese exists because it is possible to make milk coagulate. Rennet, the second ingredient, is what makes that happen.

Cheese is so familiar it's easy to overlook the fact that it's only possible because milk will separate into a solid and a liquid. Not many liquids will do that – you can't get a solid out of orange juice. If the coagulation of milk by rennet was discovered today it would be hailed as a major biotechnological breakthrough. It is quite a sophisticated process. But cheese was discovered ten thousand years ago. Pharaohs were buried with the stuff.

Rennet is an enzyme that is produced in stomachs and animal stomachs were used as milk containers. There have even been serious attempts to make human cheese, including a group at Oxford University, but no one had ever been able to get mothers' milk to split into curds and whey, except babies. When babies are sick, they are sick cottage cheese.

'Or sometimes you can use acid as well,' he said and waved the lemon. 'We'll need plenty of pigs, as well,' he continued. 'So we can feed them all the whey.' Whey is the main waste product of cheese making and there is nothing pigs like more, apart from apples. I had to pause for breath. It was all getting better and better. I felt things would never be this good again but Crudgie was teeing up his punchline. 'Then you need a bacterium. A bug,' he said. And he paused. 'I once saw a goat being milked into a pail. It was in the Pyrenees many years ago.' He paused. I said, 'Er, wow.' 'Yes, at one point in the process the goat produced a fresh steaming turd.' He was speaking very slowly now with emphasis on every word. 'The shepherd gathered it, gently, and gave it a little squeeze above the pail. So that a little bit of juice … came out … into the milk.' 'Eww, why?' I said. 'Bacteria – you've got to have 'em.'

He said that it was one of the best cheeses he'd ever tasted. They used to make Roquefort by wandering around the caves it ripened in, banging mouldy loaves of bread together, but not to worry because nowadays most bacteria were also available freeze-dried. Developing our own microbes was something we should look at, though, but we could make a pretty good soft spread with plain natural yoghurt bacteria, straight off the shelf.

Laying hands on the ingredients appeared straightforward. You still had to know what to do to them, but there wasn't really anything to be scared of. Especially if we pasteurised. A hundred years ago, everyone within twenty miles would have known how to make cheese. It was just a way of preserving surplus milk to stop it spoiling.

You could let the whey from the curds drain off naturally for instant fresh cheese or you could take the basic curds and turn them into myriad variations on a theme. Wherever there is a different word for cheese there is a different thing for cheese. Cheese means Cheddar. 'Fromage' means 'cheese' but it's something else altogether in France – never Cheddar, usually Camembert. Fromaggio probably means mozzarella or Parmesan. If you ask for 'Queso' in Spain you're most likely to get Manchego, and so it goes on and on.

Cheddar is actually one of the most sophisticated: ripe at three months, mature after nine months and vintage at twice that. Some cheeses are aged for even longer. I'd tried Hubblekäse in Zermatt. That was the oldest I've heard of – twelve years. In general, the older they get, the more dry and waxy, like Parmesan, they become. Actually, the Hubblekäse was a bit like eating a candle. Like wine, they don't go on improving forever.

The more I thought about it, the more excited I got. It was like when I learned how to play 'Whole Lotta Love' on the guitar. I thought: I can definitely do this, I really want to do this.

Cheese is universal. You could take a piece into the lost tribes of the Peruvian jungle and it'd be all you'd need to start a party. Anyone can take pleasure in the stuff. It is simple, natural and flavoursome. When you buy it, it's ready. You don't have to cook it, or peel it, or wash it and it's the tastiest thing there is. There is nothing tastier. Nothing compares to cheese for intensity of flavour, variety of flavour, depth of flavour.

After a couple of hours we were still yammering away. The milk had separated into blancmangey bits and a liquid: curds and whey. He strained the whole lot very gently through a tea towel. And there, looking totally convincing, was a little mass of proto-cheese. He said salting the surface would help to draw out more moisture and make the cheese denser. It would taste much better for hanging in the tea towel for a couple of days. But there was no question of waiting. He gave it a dusting of salt and pepper. I found a loaf of bread and a bottle of cider.

It was delicious. Smelly cheeses tend to be the most talked about, but mild ones can be just as good, more like really extravagant creamy butter.

I said, how come I've never had anything like this before? The more I thought about unusual cheese, the more I liked it, the more I wanted some. Roger was middle-aged, kind of cheesemaker shaped. He didn't look like a rock star but that's what he was. An indie hero.

We decided there and then that we'd give it a go. I cut a deal with Crudgie so he could take over the old dairy barn; there was no complicated machinery to speak of. Some things seem to get harder and harder, sometimes you try and you push and you shove and nothing happens. Sometimes you just need to say 'OK then, let's go' and all kinds of good things are happening straight away. Blackham and the gang set to work.

It was busy in the sheds, already. We were pretty much at capacity. Those sheds might not have been beautiful but they were useful. I was looking after some pregnant cows for a neighbouring farmer over the winter months. They huddled together in a cloud of huffing and blowing body heat. They spent half their time trying to escape and the other half trying to get back inside. There were sheep all over the place on the other side of the shed, cosy in the hay. Robins fluttered in and out.

We were just beginning to reel in the subtle but overwhelming buoyancy of spring. Suddenly there was nothing finer than to wander and dawdle in the gentle sun where everything was pretty: a forgotten blessing. Lambs out in the fields, lambs everywhere in fact. The cheap, modern electric fences that most farmers use didn't contain the babies at all. They ran underneath the wires, spilling out of the enclosures onto the paths and tracks, bouncing high and scattering madly as I drifted past. They are too small to inflict any damage on anything, and won't stray too far from their mothers anyway, a harmless and chaotic carnival of youth at the end of the garden.

It was a delicious and delicate thing the long, long kiss of spring. Initially nothing to compete with the high-octane confected thrills of city life but once felt, the spectacle of nature was quite addictive. Beyond the cultivated areas of the farm it was even prettier and more compelling. The newborn livestock bore more resemblance to wild animals. These are all quicker, leaner, more acutely involved with the surroundings. A fully-grown, fattened sheep is about as practical and sensible as Humpty-Dumpty. Perhaps that is why they aren't given credit for much intelligence. They don't really need any. They lived a carefree wandering, dawdling existence, eating and bleating happily all day.

I came over the crest of the hill beyond the house, out of the brilliant afternoon sunshine into the cool woods. I've never seen so many deer: hosts of timid, clever wild animals thronging the carpet of green. I realised that I'd settled down and found my place, but I was still a deer in the woods, not a sheep in the garden.

There was always something trying to move in on the farm's space, someone trying to move a footpath or cut down a forest and replace it with concrete and caravans. It was quite a lot of work just defending the borders. There was a yellow planning application notice posted near the top of the drive. I thought 'What now?' My heart was racing as I pulled over to read it. I'd really had enough of all this kind of thing. It said notice was hereby given that somebody wanted to build a cheese workshop and I realised that it was actually my own planning application. It felt good. I was pleased Paddy had used the word workshop. Everybody said, 'Don't call it a factory. Call it a workshop. The planners don't like factories. They are scared of them.' I'm not sure what the correct term is, maybe 'cave' would have sounded better. Anyhow we'd picked the right spot. When the digger went in and started hacking up the floor of the barn it uncovered an old sunken milking parlour. It had been filled in with rubble and covered with concrete. The last generation of farmers were so liberal with concrete. If I didn't get planning permission I could carry on anyway by saying, 'I'm not making cheese, it's just milk and I'm keeping some parts of it, in my old milking parlour.'

Planning permission was a formality, building regulations were a drag, but the thing I was really concerned about was the smells. There are a lot of smells wafting around the countryside. Smells are one of the great pleasures of life away from built-up areas and people were very sensitive about them.

There was a famous smell that had made the front page of all the parish publications. Daylesford's state of the art organic pickle plant had caused red-faced rage in the village. The letters page of the very local newspaper dealt exclusively with the subject for three consecutive issues. Much of the correspondence amounted to incitement to riot. Nose pollution was a serious issue.

I was in my shed looking at 'Moorlands Cheesemakers' catalogue: 'Everything for the aspiring DIY cheese enthusiast'. I was happier than I had been for a long time, filled with purpose and industry, when I became increasingly aware of a bad niff – it was off the scale. First, I thought I was mistaken but no, it was definitely there all right, more powerful than before and suddenly as big and solid as a moon. It had been worse than a bad dishcloth to start with and by the time it was in full flow it was beyond any previous benchmark of bad smells.

It was impossible to think about anything, especially cheese, with that going on, so I went in search of the source. On the far side of the yard, there was a man in a mini digger with a special attachment making a huge pile of horse muck. A couple of pregnant mares had been staying in one of the other barns. You either muck them out daily, or you put loads of straw bedding on the stable floor and keep topping it up with fresh stuff. Horse manure is one of the least offensive of the manures, but this was six months' worth and when it hit the sunlight it was properly steaming with all kinds of active chemistry. It was a pile I could think of no immediate use for. It all goes back on the fields eventually, but I still had a good hundred tonnes of cowpats that came with the place. They were pretty noxious below the crust to start with. It was like the centre of the earth in there, molten and incredibly hot but now it'd had a while to calm down it almost smelled pleasant. I must confess, I'd actually come to quite enjoy the faint whiff of sheep's business on the breeze.

That stench was easy to find but sometimes they could be quite hard to pin down. There was a really bad one in the office. Compared to the cheese factory, which was flying up in no time, Claire's office took ages to design and cost an absolute fortune. It was a saga, a steady stream of disappointments, antique oak frustrations and leather-covered foul-ups. I just gave up on having drawers in there in the end. Another mistake had been trying to hide all the wires. You always need so many wires in an office. It's amazing how many wires you need for wireless broadband, and they all have to go in the office. It was still a complete mess in there and a continual source of headaches. And just as it was nearly finished one of the cats decided to start using it as a toilet. It was a particularly bad smell that one, in a particularly sensitive spot. I couldn't trace it, even with the torch. I checked behind the computer and the radiator, all the shelves. Nothing showed up. It got worse and worse as the days went by, and became the main talking point in the household. The cleaners went in with their Marigolds but it eluded them. Claire had a theory that there were mice living there. Grandparents carried out their own separate investigations but still it lingered on. Some days it was worse than others. We'd been concentrating our search efforts on the days when the aroma was most pungent, thinking our noses would lead us to the source, but there was only a mildly nauseating hum the day that Claire found a dead rabbit under a pile of film scripts. It was most satisfying.

There are plenty of nice scents around, too, but they do tend to be more fleeting and faint than the stinks. I began to wonder just how cheesey it was going to get.

There were workmen whistling around every corner. I'd been watching them from the window and then I couldn't resist it any longer, I joined in with the decorators. Putting paint on things was calming. It smelled nice. Soon I was whistling too. It was all done in next to no time and became the first thing I showed visitors. I was immensely proud of it and I could see the neighbours who had swimming pools wishing they had built cheese workshops instead when they saw it.

*   *   *

Until we started trying to make the stuff on the farm, I thought of myself as something of a cheese expert. As far as I was concerned, I knew everything there was to know about cheese. I began to meet cheese people, people who actually did know a lot about it. People who had spent their whole working lives thinking about it: other cheese-makers, cheesemongers, cheese buyers, cheese affineurs, cheese consultants, judges. I didn't meet a single person I didn't like. Even the buyers for the big retail chains were well-informed cheese fanatics. It seemed there was a finely-tuned fraternity with its ear close to the ground for any rumbles of breaking cheese news. It all felt really good. The smallish scale of the country's independent cheesemakers was part of the joy. It was just like the indie music scene twenty years earlier. They supported each other. They all had their own niches and were more interested in creating variety and quality than competing directly with each other. In a world of mass-market homogeneity, where everything is becoming more and more the same, cheese stood out as something that was becoming more and more different. People seemed willing to go to great lengths for fine cheese.

In a puzzlingly serendipitous development it turned out that the national Cheese Awards was to be held in the field between the farm and the village and I was invited to judge. It was a huge tent, full of cheese and the massed ranks of the country's leading aficionados. I was paired up with an elderly Welsh lady, a fifth-generation cheesemaker, who really put my scant knowledge into perspective. It was instantly obvious that she was special. You never know when your next encounter with genius is going to be. Expertise is so glamorous. It can make the most mundane things fascinating. She could sniff a mild Cheddar, rub it in her fingers, have a tiny nibble and deconstruct all its qualities before I could say, 'Wow, you're absolutely right about that last one.'

We'd been nibbling our way through various Cheddars and poking at Red Leicesters all morning when something caught her eye. She nudged my arm. 'This'll be good,' she said. She knew just by looking, from the texture of the rind, from the colour, the mould. Years of experience told her that it was going to be something usually good, and it was. It was the nicest cheese I've ever tasted. There was no question about it. I'd eaten rather a lot of cheese by that time, more than I'd ever eaten before. I was practically in a dream state, but I kept going back to check that I wasn't dreaming, having another sip of apple juice and another sliver. It was always there, the same feeling. It was drug like. Ecstasies of flavour, acidity that drew moisture into my mouth, saltiness I craved and long lingering reminders. Word soon got around about that cheese and soon it was drawing a crowd. There was nothing left of it by the end of the day, just a pile of crumbs. The judging was done blind with the results announced at a later date, so I had absolutely no idea what it was called.

I was allowed to take one cheese home with me, so I grabbed as many as I could carry and struggled to the car with them. Including the second nicest cheese of the day, the second nicest one I'd ever tasted. I took it to dinner the next night and it brought the house down but all I could think about was that pile of crumbs. Once you've had the best, it's the only thing that will do. Making OK cheese isn't very difficult. Like most things, it's fairly easy to write an OK song but writing an excellent song is difficult. Making an excellent cheese is kind of tricky, too, and that was all I wanted to do.

There had been many cheese success stories of recent years. The entire country was in the throes of a gastronomic revolution and cheese was on the crest of the wave. Stichelton, Stinking Bishop, Golden Cenarth, Tunworth, Cornish Blue: all brilliant cheeses and their scarcity was part of their value. When Charles Martel rebuilt his Stinking Bishop workshop, he built it smaller than it had been before. He didn't want to expand. Demand outstripped the supply but these were all artisan products and difficult to mass produce. All the Grands Crus of the handmade cheese firmament are more or less alive, and their natural environment is a cave. That's about as far away from a supermarket shelf as you can get. I got to know lots of cheese people. They all shared their knowledge. People who trained cheesemakers, people who ran delicatessens, all the experts I could lay my hands on.

I'd restored the barn for Crudgie, but he was certainly taking his time: he was still deciding exactly what sort of cheese to make. By this point, the word was out. I was being stopped in the street by people who wanted to know where they could buy my cheese. Something had changed. Nobody wanted to know about Blur any more. They wanted to know where the cheese was.

I started working on cheese recipes with people who really knew their stuff. The recipe is the tricky part. Cheese recipes are closely guarded secrets that can change hands for vast sums. Once you've got a killer recipe you're well on your way.

We played around with milk. I had never considered how complex milk is. We brought in Marion. I didn't know how much there was to know about milk until I met Marion. Its endless complexity only became apparent after spending half an hour with her. She was an award-winning goats' cheese expert. She collected cows, too. She messed around with curds and whey in a soup kettle in Bisley, while I pickled cheese in the shed. Pickled cheese was an interesting area. I started working with fresh cheeses and pickling them because they were the most interesting things to make quickly. I just wanted to get some cheese out there in the world. We pickled it in oil, pickled it in brine, in vinegar, in eau de vie, in more or less anything, actually. I was having great fun and my goodness it was delicious, some of it – some of it was disgusting. There was one that I soaked in vinegar that was so horrible I can still taste it now. It was obviously quite poisonous, it looked nasty and it tasted rotten but even cheese that tasted nice could still be deadly. I found it hard to believe that cheese could kill, but it was true. It would be easy to create a deadly cheese by mistake so there was a painful period of waiting for the cheese to be independently tested and analysed in the laboratory.

* * *

When I wasn't looking at cheese, I was still spending a lot of time gazing at the heavens. Jupiter was spectacular one night. Every time I found Jupiter, which was always by accident, and not very often, I wondered what Galileo must have felt like when he copped it for the first time through the telescope. It was illegal to think that there was anything in the universe that didn't revolve around the earth when he invented the telescope, and he was locked up for explaining what he'd seen. When you see Jupiter through a telescope it's very clearly got moons floating around it, sharp pin pricks of light, like it's set with jewels. Even now that it's a well-known and much better understood place, to see it clearly with my own eyes was always a shocker. I started to collect great moments in human understanding and cherish them. Galileo suddenly realising that the earth was not the centre of everything. Newton suddenly understanding for certain that everything in the universe was in motion. That was maybe the most amazing split second in history; the moment when he knew for sure that the entire cosmos was actually in motion. Everyone else thought the heavens were static. Maybe Hubble felt even better than Newton when he had his moment. He noticed that the further away things are from us in space, the faster they are moving. Using very simple maths he was able to show that if you turn the clocks back, everything gets closer and closer together until about ten billion years ago they were all at a single point, and that was where space and time began.

* * *

I was woken up by the fire alarm. I'd been wondering if it worked. I'd been boning up on cosmology, and in bed the night before I'd just reached the part of the story where Hubble realises the universe is a billion times bigger than anyone had thought. It made me feel very hungry and clever, and I'd popped downstairs for a midnight cheesey crumpet. When the alarm woke us up at 6 a.m., the house was thick with acrid smoke. I sprang out of bed and ran around looking for the fire screaming, 'Get the babies! Get the babies!' It was hard to tell where the smoke was coming from, because it was everywhere. I had come to my senses, but my brain was still booting up. It finally flickered to life and said 'Crumpets!' The whole grill was glowing red and had set fire to the shelf above it. It's hard to say how long it was from eyes open to fire blanket flapping, probably less than twenty seconds. Another couple of minutes and the flames would have licked through the ceiling.

It was hard enough to put the thing out as it was. The chunky shelf was well and truly detonating, it had been toasted so dry that it refused to stop smouldering and reigniting despite half a dozen stockpots full of water. I put the oven gloves on, wrenched the whole thing off the wall and hurled it in the fireplace.

It was such a horrible smell, toxic and bitter. It took ages to find the keys that open all the different window locks, but once the windows were all thrown open, the stench was gone in an hour or so. The shelf was still burning away merrily in the grate. I've rarely fallen asleep feeling as clever as I did, with my head full of cosmological constants. I've never woken up and felt so stupid. It was a close squeak.

I'm hardly in Hubble's league but I did seem to have actually made some quite nice cheese and I felt rather good about it. I certainly know how Linda McCartney felt when she created the world's first frozen vegetarian sausage. Making cheese and making music are obviously completely different but the results are equally satisfying. Being in a band involved having my photograph taken often. To make cheese I needed to wear a plastic hat, plastic bag slippers and a white paper coat and if I hadn't shaved I had to put a weird thing over my beard as well.

I liked it the way clothes had a completely different function in the countryside. Not just work clothes. Fashion was usually forsaken for the sake of practicality in these rural scenarios. Something with a bit of mud on it was not necessarily dirty. Pockets, really big ones, were always an asset. Trainers were hopeless. Strangely, in the total absence of fashion values, people's clothes tended to express their personalities far more acutely than anywhere else.

I doubt if anyone for miles around even had an inkling what London Fashion Week was. Pulling on a big work boot gave me more of a feeling of confidence and all-conquering majesty than any other shoe I could ever remember. When you've got the right gear on, winter is a picnic. There were no tourists, even in Daylesford, but it was every bit as beautiful in February as it was in August.

Everything was springing to life. The days were getting longer. There were thousands of snowdrops, here, there and everywhere. Everything was regenerating and even though I was working harder than ever it still felt like being on holiday.

SPRING

CHAPTER 7

MUSIC

Up at half past four. Everyone dreads getting up that early but rising with the lark is probably the cheapest and most certain way to feel glamorous. The utter silence of the middle of the night in the middle of the winter, that stillness coupled with the early riser's sense of purpose; the promise of things about to happen was exhilarating. There is no sunshine like early March sunshine. It is rare and there is only the tiniest amount of warmth in it but the colour was like a magic spell. It gave a sense of hope to the huge amounts of devastation underway. The whole farm was getting a haircut. Hedges trimmed, the digger was back in commission and hoiking out overgrown trees. I hardly recognised the place. It was definitely going to look amazing in fifty years.

*   *   *

The next-door farmer was retiring after a lifetime spent in the fields and the sheds. He was selling everything he had, from his piles of rubble to his shiny mini tractor. I went for a poke around. Mud is something I'd avoided for most of my life, but I was making up for lost time. It seemed to be the main ingredient of agriculture. It is pretty miraculous stuff, mud. You can make all kinds of things out of it if you get the right machines and the right mixture.

All the equipment was laid out in rows in one of the fields. There was a lot of it, an entire career's worth. It told a story but it was hard to tell which bits were junk and which were vital to the plot. I recognised some tractor-type things and there were some iron gates in a pile but it was quite hard to tell exactly what anything else was. The brochure said there was a pig-slaughtering stool, but I couldn't find that. There were a few muddy people around staring at things. One of them, a big fat one, did an enormous burp in my ear as I walked past. He just carried on staring out from his benign, muddy, burp world. People in the country are much madder than in the city. Close contact with massed humanity does keep your feet on the ground. Being at the centre of nothing but a distant three-hundred-and-sixty-degree horizon all day, I guess you get used to doing whatever you like. This guy would have made the Dean Street crack muffins look clean and reasonable if you'd put them side by side. It wasn't a threatening burp, in fact the bizarreness of it put me quite at ease: the strain of the vast silence between strangers, from quite different worlds, meeting in a field, relieved by a belch. It was as if he'd burped for both of us.

I'd been looking forward to the sale and, as I'd suspected I would, I wanted to buy everything. Especially the stuff that looked old and well used. If it had worked here for a lifetime, presumably it would go on working next door for a while longer. Even though I had my hands full with cheese, and Fred had the fields under control, I still wanted to try as many different things as possible. There was cider-making equipment, there were staddle stones, whatever they are, old wagon wheels and mangles, an ancient tractor. All sorts of treasure. Everyone was there. Paddy and all his gang, Fred and Gwynne. Blackham. It was an auspicious occasion. It was like being at a music festival, but the food was really good – bacon rolls. Paddy said I definitely shouldn't buy any tractors, but I saw him eyeing up a nice old blue one. Quite a lot of people had actually come to the auction in their tractors. I'd started to really like old tractors. I think any man who saw one standing pretty in a field with a For Sale sign on it, would be tempted to dream for a moment. They speak to all men. They are slow, simple things in a fast and complicated world. There is nothing about an old tractor that can't be fixed with an oily rag and an adjustable wrench and somehow the cheaper and older they are, the more appealing they become. Fred had an appalling old heap that was forever conking out, but he never gave up on it. He didn't have a dog. He had that tractor. The crappy blue one went to a dealer for four grand, which was more than we all thought, but there were some bargains in the sprayer section. I had to leave before the corn crusher went under the hammer, because I was due to spend the day writing songs with Kevin Rowland, the singer from Dexy's Midnight Runners, but I've been thinking about it ever since.

It was an inspiring morning all round. I decided to invite all the surrounding farmers round for some lamb, and to show them my drainage system, which I was quite proud of. They struck me as a contented group of people. Fred always had a bonfire going and a big grin on his face. Nature's bounty seemed to rub off. Resourcefulness pervades in farmyards. Things get repaired with other things that are lying around. My first inclination was to make everything beautiful, but I soon came to realise that there is a lot to be said for bodging. A good bodge-up is a triumph of individualism. One of the hay barns was made from hacked-up telegraph poles and bent railway tracks with a roof of old planks with nails sticking out. My first thought was to knock it down and make a proper one, but I've realised that it is, in fact, a proper one, and now it's falling down and I'm thinking about how to restore it.

When most of this farm was built in the 1800s, agriculture was lucrative, booming like the music business of the 1980s. The money generated from farming was sufficient to finance ambitious construction projects. There was little in the way of building regulations or planning permission, but the quality and visual appeal of the agricultural buildings trumped anything built in recent years. Sumptuous stone and slate barns flew up left, right and centre, chasing productivity, to house and process all kinds of crops: grain, milk, livestock. Back then the value of the farm was in the value of its output, not locked up in the value of the buildings. Nowadays, a small 200-acre farm like the one I called home generated trifling amounts of cash, and those resplendent but redundant outbuildings, monuments to another era, were probably its most valuable assets.

Running the farm made me the ruler of a small kingdom. It was an expensive country to live in. As well as Paddy, I needed a farm accountant, a bookkeeper and various solicitors with expertise in different areas of the law. There was always some rotter trying to pull a fast one on one of my borders. The boundaries were where the majority of skirmishes took place, but within the realm, things were pretty complicated, too. The farm was populated by ever-increasing numbers of barn builders, sheep ticklers, cow stokers and cheese freaks. They all needed to be on payrolls. There was an ever-increasing amount of paperwork. I had to speak to the accountant all the time. Strangely, as I discovered I was losing my ability to get excited about the Top 40 singles, I found accountants, lawyers and plumbers more and more interesting.

Even when Blur were the biggest band in Britain I always used to leave meetings at the accountant's feeling slightly deflated. Getting old is expensive. Recently, accounts meetings were borderline humiliating. My accountant was always trying to be helpful. 'We look after the act that came third in *X Factor*, you know they're doing phenomenally well. They had two number ones last year, I can get you the manager's phone number if you like,' or nodding towards the newly installed Gorillaz multi-platinum disc behind his desk and suggesting, 'It's a real shame that Blur don't re-form and do a few shows.' I went and picked him up from the station on the quad bike, possibly a mistake, as his shoes were shiny and the quad bike was muddy. It was a busier day than most, too. There was a lot of tree planting and fencing happening.

It promised to be a particularly tricky meeting because the farm was struggling to make a profit. Most businesses take a while to start making money. Farms have to be profitable within five years trading or the Inland Revenue start to think you're just messing around, rather than running a business. It's quite serious. They can take away your tractor, everything if they think you're just enjoying yourself setting cheese on fire and staring at sunsets.

Looking at the row of figures that represented actual farm income caused me to reflect on how far the pendulum has swung. It is very difficult to make money from agriculture in the twenty-first century. Turning the decaying farm buildings, magnificent structures that were all erected without a single form being filled in, into useable things took endless negotiating with planners, building regulators and accountants, but it appeared I was winning. At least I hadn't lost any money in the last twelve months. We'd made a tiny profit. I fairly floated around after that meeting, in higher spirits than during the Britpop goldrush.

*   *   *

The music business was in a far more precarious state than agriculture. Archaeological discoveries from the end of the ice age show music is as much a part of our development as food and shelter, but the record companies' business model was failing. It was getting harder and harder to make money out of records but music will never go away, no matter what happens. Today it is impossible to go and buy a loaf of bread without hearing Coldplay or Lady Gaga, but there is a whole new generation who've grown up without paying for music. I don't know if making it free makes it sound better. Making food free never made it taste any nicer, either. It was causing problems up the chain and the big old battleship-type recording studios were lying as empty and useless as the threshing barn.

Until just before we arrived, there had been a recording studio in Chippy. Some of my favourite records had been recorded there. 'Baker Street' by Gerry Rafferty, Duran Duran's first album, The Smiths and The Bay City Rollers had been regulars: practically all my favourite bands had been there and meted out the troy weight of their 22-carat genius. I still had the entire collection of records I'd bought while I was growing up. There were only about fifty of them, but I knew all the words to all of them and I recognised every scratch. I can remember where I bought every single one of them, and who I was with at the time. I had all my grandad's records and all my dad's, and I still listened to them. Ray Conniff's big band bonanzas, light music, Eddie Hawkins, Leadbelly.

I've outgrown a lot of things I thought I'd love forever: books, habits, hobbies, houses, friends, even whole countries, but the music I loved and lived in when I was young, I will take to my grave. Songs that came out when I was a teenager, even songs I hated by bands I didn't like back then, filled me with nostalgia and pride when I heard them now. 'The Sun Always Shines on TV' by A-ha came on the radio. I didn't care for it at the time but now it gave me goose pimples. I never stopped listening to music or playing music. I didn't listen to much new stuff. I went the other way, upstream, to the music that the bands that I'd always liked were influenced by. It was easy to find on YouTube. I knew the Beatles like I knew my times tables. I found out that they liked Roy Orbison and I started listening to Roy a lot. He made me shiver. I wandered around the woods singing 'Dream Baby' at the top of my voice. Roy was only a stone's throw from being an opera singer, really, an operatic tenor. That's how I arrived, step-by-step via the Beatles and Roy, in a world of music I never thought I'd have anything to do with: the realms of the orchestra. I remembered liking the William Tell Overture when I was young. I put it on, really loud one morning. I was in tears by the end. I just couldn't believe how brilliant it was. Pop music is the heartbeat of cities, but in the countryside violas and French horns really kicked it.

Stephen Street, who had produced all the Blur albums, was the coolest man in town again. He came down and played me the new Pete Doherty album he'd been working on. I could tell it had driven him mad. We went out for dinner and talked about the good old days. We talked about microphones. I found I was much more interested in the technical side of music now. I explained what microphones I'd been using on the drumkit, and was pleased that he agreed with my thinking. We sat up in the studio listening to Kool and the Gang, and Eddie Harris records much later than we'd ever stayed up before. Then he picked up a guitar and started playing 'Every Day Is Like Sunday', a song he'd written with Morrissey. I joined in on the double bass and then we were both singing our heads off. Those impromptu moments are the most enjoyable of all. Winning Brit awards, falling out of Rolls Royces, people screaming: it's nothing compared to the feeling of music.

Music is academia, really: its own greatest reward. There were loads of local bands. Rock bands, ensembles, choirs, an operatic society. The Chipping Norton Silver Band were my favourite: a brass band that were so huge that they usually outnumbered their audience. Most people walked right past, others stood there and talked all the way through it. They can't have taken more than a few quid all afternoon, you'd get paid more doing a paper round. The composer arrived by bicycle, rather than by Bentley, and he looked a bit like a monk. They had three tuba players. That's more than an orchestra. They performed outside the Co-op with their gloves and coats on, like poor church mice. The children hated it and said it was too loud, one of them threw his gingerbread man to the ground in protest, but the sound of a gigantic brass band was one to relish.

Maybe we don't need rock stars quite so much now that we have celebrities. As long as Chippy has a big band, it really doesn't bother me.

I had a symphony orchestra in my laptop, a guitar in my phone. Technology had made everything cheaper and easier. Fifteen years ago, a state of the art recording studio would have cost well over a million pounds. Mix consoles were vast and needed continuous maintenance by ex-NASA scientists. Even a pair of the requisite two-inch tape machines with Dolby could cost more than a house. Studios featured endless corridors of doors that led to specially designed rooms housing reverb plates, power supplies and air conditioning units. You had to have A/C to offset the heat generated by miles of hot circuitry buzzing in the heavily insulated soundproofed chambers. The A/C systems were so sophisticated they went wrong more than anything else and caused all kinds of problems of their own. The cost of investing in all that equipment – allegedly more than a million pounds on doors alone at Air Studios – meant that decent studios were only to be found in the nicer parts of town where the buildings were worth investing in: St John's Wood, Primrose Hill, Soho, Bloomsbury, Fulham, Hampstead. Making a record had been like boarding a luxury cruise liner with bar, brasserie and legions of helpful staff. It was just the beginning of an out of control spiral of spending that meant that a record company's profit margin on a CD that cost £13.99, was about the same as it had been on a piece of vinyl that had cost £4.99 ten years previously.

I am proud to have been a part of that madness. It's hard to see how it could have been avoided. Recording costs were nothing compared to marketing budgets. If everyone else was spending a hundred thousand quid on a video, there was nothing record companies could do but stump up the cash. It was a buoyant market and nobody minded. How things had changed. All the technology disappeared inside a telephone. All that was needed now to make a record were six microphones and an idea of where to put them. I'd had to invest in more gear in order to make a handmade cheese than a record.

We'd crossed that lovely line in the diary where it was just warmer outside than in and we didn't have to close doors behind us any more. Spring always takes me by surprise. It's hard to say which way it's going to roll with the weather in March. Can't tell. One day it's so grey, wet and windy it's hard to recall how balmy it was two days before. Then it was all clear skies and forever, and we could walk the fields without wellingtons: the kids squeaking with delight, exploring a previously inaccessible patch of woodland, an overgrown spinney that I'd just put a gate in.

Suddenly, the endless complications of living on a farm all made simple, straightforward sense: the big machine we lived in was paying out one of its occasional jackpots. Beguiling scenery, the enchantment of transporting smells, the weather all of a sudden, overwhelming. The thrill of the throb of nature was more than enough for now. Where else would I want to be?

The grass was so green in early March it was lurid, practically psychedelic. You could tell everything in the ground was on the point of exploding but the conifers, the evergreens, were the richest, deepest, most soothing colour, a mesmerising colour, like a mantra. Later on, it was utterly silent in the ancient field called Bank. As I came down the hill at a jog, quite alone, tripping over the undulating ridges and furrows, lost in my thoughts, I caught sight of a heron unfolding itself, not with the startled panic of a deer, but calm and statesmanlike. An unexpectedly exotic creature, the colour of liquid steel, stretching its wings and walking up an invisible ladder to settle at the very tip of a Scots pine.

It was lovely but there was work to be done. I now had more jobs than I'd ever had in the rest of my life put together. The trouble with making music is that it can be hard to tell when you're working and when you're messing around. I learned how to play the mandolin and the ukulele – the shed was home to more and more musical instruments. It was always tempting to spend a few minutes hugging a euphonium or tickling a trumpet. It's impossible to look back at time spent playing music, no matter how silly it is, and consider it anything other than time well spent.

Ukuleles are the musical equivalent of those pedalo boats that you can hire by the hour on French beaches. You always look a little bit silly when you are on one but when you're actually in there doing it, you can't really go wrong.

There's nothing to it, and it feels good no matter what anyone else might think.

Ukuleles and their forgotten cousins banjoleles and bandolins, were having a renaissance, maybe because it is impossible to play a ukulele without smiling. There are no laments or dirges in the entire canon of ukulele compositions, and with the possible exception of the electric bass guitar, it's the closest anyone has come to making a musical apparatus that anyone can get to grips with in about twenty minutes.

The euphonium was a trickier instrument to steer: more like manoeuvring a punt than a pedalo. It had to be approached standing right at the back and aimed at very carefully, anticipating corners well in advance. Large brass instruments will never be fashionable, but they ran in the James family like big ears. We all had them.

I was beginning to think that all bands ended up hating each other. The Rolling Stones didn't appear to like each other very much. Roger Daltry and Pete Townshend seemed to need each other more than like each other. Certain members of Pink Floyd appeared to loathe each other more than the parties in a messy divorce.

It made me think there wasn't much hope for Blur. I couldn't think of a single band who liked each other a little bit. Even rubbish bands split up and hated each other.

One of the benefits of being in Blur was that I got to meet my heroes. Whoever said you should never meet your heroes must have been really boring. He must have really bored his hero to death to elicit such a disappointing reaction. Bernard Sumner was my hero.

I remember I first heard his band, New Order's, biggest hit 'Blue Monday' on the telephone. There were 'Hit Hotlines', numbers that played crackly music down the line at exorbitant rates. The boy who I sat next to at school had been talking about 'Blue Monday' a lot, so I called the number for it. It was like telephoning a dream. It was dancey. It was long, slightly menacing. I heard it again at the under-eighteens disco.

It was a spectacularly grey piece of music, but uplifting like a February sky. I bought a copy and listened to it so much I completely wore it out. It was unusual, but simple enough to copy and I learned how to play every part. I didn't have music lessons but I had that record and it had taught me everything I'd needed to know. Then I started listening to New Order's other records, and Joy Division, their earlier incarnation, and that was when I knew wanted to be in a band.

Bernard and his bass player had fallen out, too. I talked to Bernard about Blur. He said, 'Oh this is only the first time you've split up. It's much worse the second time.' Bernard came over a few times and the first time we got drunk he said, 'Let's record a few tracks then.' He came back with a drummer and a guitar player and some microphones and before I knew what was happening the house was full of my favourite band and I'd become the bass player.

There were microphones and amplifiers humming every-where, in sheds, courtyards, stables. We bashed down seven songs in two days. It went really well.

The strange thing was how irritating I found it, having the best band ever living in the house. The place got so untidy. There was all the washing up, the laundry. You should definitely meet your heroes but I'd avoid having them come and live at your house.

There were a lot of guitarists hanging around the farm at the time. Bill had a couple of Australian guys staying with him. He brought them round. It was raining and I was trying to fix a leak. One of them held the ladder. They were on tour. They'd just played the Wigmore Hall in London and they were off to Vladivostok next. I made them carrot soup. Bill took me to one side and whispered 'They're the two best classical guitarists in the world.' There is no stick for measuring music with, but those boys, who were brothers, seemed to have specially designed fingers. They were long fingers like spiders, nothing like my bangers. It was raining quite heavily by the time they got down to playing anything. It had taken them ages to settle down. They'd been intrigued by the euphonium and the cello, and especially by the 'hyper-fuzz' pedal Bernard had left behind. Everybody liked that one. It was an ice-breaker.

They plugged in a couple of guitars. One of them said that they didn't play electric guitar, really. Well, that was a lie. The rain kept coming down. Their playing made the rain immaculate. They were the best guitarists I've ever heard. Music so beguiling that the years fell away, and I was floating in perfect timeless space again. If I had to pick one word to describe the sound they made, it would be 'clean'. Everything about it was clear and pure.

Whenever I work with a singer for the first time, I never know quite what to expect. It's never the same twice anyway but, to complicate things, quite a lot of famous singers, including my favourite male and favourite female vocalist, don't know one end of a scale from the other. They just sing. Some singers know exactly what they are doing and some have no idea at all.

At the age of twelve, when she was singing on the 'Fat Les' records, Lily Allen was always able to neatly lay down several harmonies and double track them, but I never heard Marianne Faithfull sing a single harmony and I don't think she's ventured above middle-C for three decades, but hers is still a great voice. Singers don't necessarily have to be great musicians. They just need to have great voices or be able to write really good words – or to look good enough to make you want to listen to them.

As a songwriter working with a singer, until you get started with them, it's never clear whether it will be a question of the two of you writing music and words together; or trotting out some music which inspires them to start singing to and writing words for; or as simple as handing them over a completely finished song.

I always quite liked the idea that someone can just naturally sing. I'm always staggered how some singers with no formal knowledge of music manage to function, as if singing is completely innate, like speech, and that it can be learned, just by listening, like any other spoken language.

I met a girl called Florence. She was at art college but it was obvious she was big trouble straight away. There was a bloke with her. Just sort of hanging round looking sappy. I said, 'Are you the machine?' and he said, 'No she's Florence *and* the Machine. I'm Johnny. Johnny Borrell from Razorlight.' He was a nice boy but you could see he didn't stand a chance with Florence. She was wearing minuscule hotpants and doing cartwheels.

I said, 'Do you like ukuleles and stuff?' She said, 'OK,' and laughed and she came to stay the next week.

It was sunny and we spent the first day floating around Daylesford and going to the pub. It's not like building fences or digging holes, writing songs. Sometimes if you start later you finish earlier. It's hard to know how to start. It's either incredibly awkward or just plain wonderful. Florence didn't play an instrument, although uniquely she liked to hold one while she was singing. It is beyond me how anyone can just sing like that. She had such a robust sense of pitch that song was as natural to her as it is to a cuckoo. She had written a ballad. She sang it to me with no accompaniment. It was perfect as it was, solo voice. So that was done. There was another one, about bees, in the bag by lunchtime. She was pacing round the shed in one direction and I was pacing in the other. I didn't know what to do so I plugged in the 335. It was like going for a ride in a Rolls Royce that guitar, it took you places. Then she was singing all of a sudden and I wonder if she'd ever sung like that before. It was like seeing something being born, she just opened up and sang her heart out. Exhilarating and obvious she was going to break a lot more hearts than Johnny's.

I was woken up in the morning by a friendly headbutt from one of the twins, as usual, and the song we'd started was in my head. That's the best reason to get up in the morning, for a song.

Biscuit arrived at lunchtime. Biscuit was the drummer and it got better and better. The studio is a shed, the same sort as the chickens live in, but it couldn't have worked any better if it had been a castle in the Bahamas.

A lawless, impossible, fleeting muse and eleven chickens in the yard.

CHAPTER 8

FOOD

The acre of concrete outside the back door of the farm-house had been used for making silage, winter feed for dairy cattle. It must have cost a fortune to put there. It had a battleship's scale and beauty, made me feel dizzy. I loved the idea of dairy cows but I didn't want to look at a mould-ering slab every time I went outside. An enormous monster of a ship on caterpillar tracks came and chewed it all up, came from Russia where it had been eating whole airports. There are still some kerbstones missing where it grazed the end of Crudgie's barn and started eating that while the driver wasn't looking. It quickly transformed a perfect plane into a perfect cone, a huge mountain of concrete pebbles that came in useful for making paths.

* * *

The concrete had been laid on a bed of clay. Really beautiful clay. I couldn't believe the farmer had gone to such an unnecessary expense until I realised that the clay was just planet earth. I hadn't just bought some fields. There was all this other stuff underneath them that came as part of the deal. I didn't just buy the perfect dream. I bought a great big slice of reality too, a piece of a planet.

Whoever laid the concrete had removed an acre of topsoil but I couldn't find where they'd put it. There was plenty of quite well rotted cow manure so I used a mixture of that, and silt dredged from the ditches and the old lake down by the railway, but I still had to buy some topsoil and it was expensive. It probably ended up costing more to lay the soil than it had to lay the concrete. I could have scraped a thin layer of earth off the fields but that seemed wrong. The value of agricultural land is really the trading value of the topsoil, the scarce few inches of the surface layer.

The farm's land had been under cultivation for centuries and everything had sprung from those miraculous inches. I hadn't realised how little of it there actually was. I became quite fascinated by the cosmic fudge of the subsoil, too, the next layer down and soon I was wondering what was underneath that. Looking through some old documents I discovered that in the thirties someone had really gone to town and had a geological core sample taken to analyse all the sub strata. There were silt belts from Jurassic seas, chalk veins, oolitic limestone strands. Layers upon layers all sitting on top of a huge magnet, a molten core of quick iron spinning through space making pretty patterns in other dimensions, strange fields that we know nothing about at all.

I replaced the concrete with a grass meadow until I knew what I wanted to do with it. Ravey Davey, the new gardener, built a kind of Stonehenge thing there on the grass. I tried telling him I didn't really want one but he wouldn't take no for an answer. 'Oh, you don't want a stone circle. OK. We'll do it square. No? OK, you win, we'll do a stone rectangle.' He spent a fortnight making a crazy paving oblong out of rubble and then left to go and work for Damien Hirst. I fired up the digger and we began to lay out the vegetable garden.

Gardens are where 'happy ever after' happens. Engrossed in scents and sunshine I wrestled with what to plant, where. It was like trying to do a lifetime's grocery shopping in a week. So many varieties of potato and species of beetroot to choose from: purple carrots, yellow cucumbers – the more out there it was, the more I liked the sound of it – salsify, scorzonera, escarole, ramsons and damsons. I tried to order some laver as well but it turned out to be a kind of seaweed.

'And land cress is a must,' I said. The new gardener looked confused. 'You know, it's like watercress, only it's land. Isn't that amazing!' The garden was a complete fantasy, and there was so much flying around in my head, I wondered for a second if I'd only dreamed about it. Cress was buried deep in Claire's subconscious, too. She had developed a fascination with green leafy salads during one of her pregnancies and it had rubbed off on me. Watercress grew wild in abundance on the farm, huge great friendly swamps of it. They were so inviting: shady pools full of salad and mineral water. I'd shrieked with delight when I'd discovered the stuff and eaten it by the handful but after raving about it to Paddy, he warned me off. Sheep often contaminate it with liver fluke, an unthinkably horrible parasite.

I wondered if we'd save money by selling the sheep in that field and concentrating on the watercress, but the more I learned about growing vegetables, the less likely that seemed. For reasons that were hard to fathom to begin with, it was more expensive to grow our own food than to buy it. Even if I paid myself minimum wage to grow high-yield tomatoes in polytunnels, it would still be cheaper to go to the supermarket in a taxi and buy the most expensive ones. But I wanted all kinds of tomatoes that weren't available in the shops and I was prepared to pay. I ordered black Russian ones, bright yellow Mexican ones, teeny tiny ones, fat purple beefy ones, long ones, stripey ones. There were so many shapes, sizes and colours. There were whole catalogues devoted to spooky tomatoes and nothing else.

I didn't have a building that was quite suitable for growing tomatoes in. It was irritating to have to build something else when there were still numerous sheds, outbuildings, stables and barns standing around that I wasn't really using for anything. Still, the greenhouse in the catalogue looked like quite good value. I ordered one and it arrived the next day. It was in ten thousand pieces. It took Blackham and

Doa about a month to build it, and they had to get their bass player, Tricksy Steve, to come and help them lay a concrete slab. Then there was all the staging for inside, and the plants. It was like building a second home.

Animals were even more ridiculous than plants. I had a pair of pedigree Gloucesters on order from the milk fanatic in Bisley. There was a long queue for Gloucesters, but now I wasn't sure if I was ready for cows after all.

It's cheaper to run aeroplanes than cattle. I'd been looking after the neighbour's pregnant cows to get a feel for it, but now they were gone and only muddy patches remained. I'd enjoyed entertaining them and every way I looked at it, it made sense to get cows. It should have worked. I was hankering after a cow. We got through a lot of milk. I had five children and a huge cappuccino machine. I lived on a dairy farm. I had sheds. I had fields. Cows aren't that expensive – they are about the same price as a suit. You can get a cheap cow for the price of a cheap suit and a fancy cow for the price of a fancy suit. Even milking machines were intriguing things and good value, but the crunch was that I'd have to milk the cow twice a day or pay someone to do it. In order to make that work I'd need to get a whole herd, and before I knew what was happening I was looking at a row of figures that went beyond what I'd ever spent on an aeroplane. The only way to make it work with dairy cows seemed to be to have 10,000 or none at all. All the agricultural shows were cancelled because of foot and mouth anyway. The sheep took a complete rest from touring and showbusiness.

The pig was ready to start breeding. She was ready for anything. Raring to go. Pigs are like that. Ever ready. Anyone who has ever worked with pigs will tell you that it takes exactly three months, three weeks and three days for a sow to produce a litter, a dozen tiny piglets. They suckle the piglets, spend a couple of weeks resting in the straw and then they're off again. I was still hanging around the pigsty in the way I'd previously hung around at The Groucho Club. On bright mornings there would be all kinds of cobwebs adorning the hay bales in the pigsty: dripping complexes of strange geometry and secrets. It was hard to tell if there would be one very large spider in the middle, or a million little ones. I could happily devote time to the intriguing world of the spider, investigating its mysteries, but as usual there was no time to dwell, the vet was coming and I wanted to make sure everything was tickety-boo in the pig department.

A pair of good wellies confers invincibility on the wearer, a sense of swagger beyond anything Savile Row can muster. I felt wonderfully connected, grounded in the real world standing in pig muck, up to my arms in huge cobwebs. The hay bales were like big packets of shredded wheat and exploded pleasingly when the twine was cut, into a shower of tickles and a comfortable sweet-scented carpet. I was throwing straw and spiders around, the pig was galloping up and down with glee, a curl in her tail, tossing clumps in the air with her snout and singing gently when the vet arrived, full of the benevolent stillness of people who spend their lives dealing with animals. He persuaded the pig and me to calm down without so much as a word.

We had to change the tag in the pig's ear, quite a simple job, but one that seemed to end up involving all hands present. Pigs attract people, the same way that spiders repel us, and everybody wanted to get involved. Pretty soon, everything else had ground to a halt and people were waving apples and chasing her, grown men falling over in the straw giggling.

One snip and it was done. 'Does she look all right, other than her ear?' I asked the vet.

'She's a fine pig,' he said. My heart filled with pride. She certainly was.

The gardener reversed the quad bike and trailer into the greenhouse and it fell over. It had been very difficult to get the quad bike to go in reverse recently, so, she pointed out, there was a silver lining but there weren't any tomatoes. The greenhouse hadn't been a success.

The ugliest thing I've ever seen is the coast of Spain, south of Barcelona. Almost the entire length of it is covered in polytunnels. Thousands and thousands and thousands of them. They must be visible from space, a kind of polythene Great Wall of China. It made me feel sick, endless ugliness stuck on the mountainsides.

That wasn't going to stop me having one. There was a biodynamic farmer on the other side of the hill and he'd won me over. I went inside his to have a look. He waved his arms around, said 'Herbs up here, pot plants down there, got to go, enjoy yourself,' nodded at a table and chairs and disappeared. It was so calm and pretty in there amongst the peppers and parsley, a brightly coloured world of its own, that I was still sitting there thinking how nice it all smelled when he came back an hour later. He sat down as well. It was so warm and cosy and it smelled so good we didn't even have to say very much. I knew I had to get one.

So much more fun than a swimming pool, slightly warmer than the world outside, and chock full of curling, climbing plants. It was like being in an aquarium, but better. Everyone should have one, I decided.

I told him about the horror show on the Spanish coast. He said he thought it was a question of degree. Covering the whole place with polythene was ridiculous but then, not taking advantage of a longer growing season didn't make much sense either.

His polytunnel was quite a nice shape, too. I wandered around the farm trying to work out where to put mine, but there really wasn't anywhere it could go without spoiling a view. The garden was taking shape and everything was starting to look quite tidy.

I was learning about farming the same way I learned most about music: by jumping in and doing it. That's probably the best way to learn anything. The boredom of the classroom is replaced by a different kind of anxiety, a combination of panic and dreadful slow-motion, close-up self-awareness. I made so many mistakes. I always have. I once started a show with the wrong guitar. It had been tuned a semitone below concert pitch. That was the worst one ever. It's hard to think of a better definition of 'mistake' than playing exactly in time exactly a semitone out of tune. I knew I was putting my fingers in the right places and the right tunes were coming out, so I soldiered on with gusto glaring at everybody else on the stage until the whole thing collapsed into silence.

Mistakes are rarely catastrophic, though. They're usually just annoying. Having messed up so many times should mean it happens less and less, but the more it happens, the less scary it is and the lack of fear leads me inevitably to further calamity. Buying the farm was the cleverest thing I ever did, which was the main thing, but I reckoned I'd probably made a mistake almost every day since. Sometimes they took months or years to mature. There were so many decisions to make. Fortunately, I had Paddy to help me. I ran everything by him. Paddy won his wisdom at the Royal Agricultural College in Cirencester, the capital of the Cotswolds. I'd often thought about taking a night school course there and I finally went there for lunch one day, at the invitation of the professor who ran it. Somehow or other, he knew Claire's horse. In a similar way that there is usually some sort of catastrophe in progress at the farm, there is always some kind of major emergency going on in the world of agriculture. Pigs in crisis, bees in decline, there's always something, but the elevating calm and splendour of the college transported me far away from my messes and dilemmas, and from the inner quadrangles it was hard to conceive of a pig farmer suffering or an evil chicken baron.

Until the previous week, I had considered buying horses the biggest mistake of my farming career. They were more expensive than houses. It cost Blur less to crash land on Mars than it did to keep Frosty and Cornflake trotting round in circles, but as I walked through the college gates I suddenly saw my investment realised. Good old Cornflake, I thought, possibly for the first time ever, for making the introduction.

The Royal Agricultural College is modelled on an Oxford college, perched at the end of a long corridor of ancient planes in beautiful grounds, and it promised to hold the answers to almost everything that interested me. The magazine section in the library alone would have kept me happy for the rest of the year. A consortium of maize specialists were in conference in the big hall: all the country's greatest maize brains gathering to share their verve for corn-on-the-cob. I was surprised at the number of girls in the canteen: many of them, too, led there by their horses. It's great when your horse romps home. Where would we be without our mistakes? They always lead us to the solution.

Lunch, discussing the price of sausage rolls in a castle stuffed with the glamour of youth and all tomorrow's hopes, was excellent. I was beginning to think that farmers held at least one or two aces. There is nothing people need more than food, nothing more precious on the market.

Musicians were no longer unique deities, just another species of celebrity, but food had suddenly become relevant. There were more television programmes about it than anything else.

I got back home more determined than ever to build a polytunnel. Three quarters of the farm buildings that clustered around the house were overflowing now. The house itself was full of children, the wooden sheds were full of livestock. There were hundreds of tonnes of last summer's hay in the towering Dutch barns. The pigsty was in business, the chicken run, too. That was now also home to several guineafowl and a goose, but there were still a couple of big concrete, steel and asbestos agricultural buildings which had always been quite under used. I hadn't found a purpose for them. I mean they were full of stuff: a broken digger, guttering, lengths of plastic tube, a trampoline, the old BMW rusting in peace and so on, but they had never had any specific purpose. They were a luxury really, those sheds. I always thought I was just lucky to have them.

It suddenly occurred to me that instead of building a polytunnel, I could just clingfilm one of those sheds and grow my tomatoes in there.

The whole ship was gathering momentum and building up a head of steam. Paddy was confident we were ready for our first crop of wheat so we put down forty acres of a variety called 'Brigadier'. I had already started to develop a mozzarella. All I needed was tomatoes and the whole farm would be an enormous pizza generator.

Clingfilming wasn't anywhere near as cheap and practical as I'd hoped but a garden centre that had gone bust on top of the hill was selling off all its old greenhouses, panel by panel. I bought the whole lot and turned the rusty old shed into a giant Crystal Palace.

I often wondered how the farm must have looked a hundred or two hundred years ago, the concreted over, walled Victorian market garden or the forty acres of ancient woodland that had been chopped down by the owner before last where the wheat was now growing. But it was the orchards that I thought about more than anything.

I began planning a new one and realised I needed Daphne, the grouse moor grandee's expert horticultural help once more. The more I thought and learned about orchards, the more I liked them. Orchards are mesmerising, their crystal symmetry perfect, otherworldly. They are cheap. They require hardly any maintenance and, for the cost of a couple of bottles of cider, they crank out fruit like magic porridge pots, year in, year out. The only bothersome bit with orchards is planning them. Each tree needs complementary pollinator species or they won't fruit and that made selecting the ideal thirty trees quite a complicated puzzle. With that many trees it was possible to have fruit more or less the whole year round. I tussled with it for ages trying to get the right balance, but the only way I could make it work was by planting more trees. So I kept on planting more trees.

* * *

The farm and I grew into each other. The serene worlds of tomato sheds and apple groves couldn't have been further from the here, there and everywhere of showbusiness. Maybe that's why they were so popular with musicians. I thought I was being quite reckless and romantic when we bought the farm on our honeymoon but I soon realised it was just another rock cliché, as inevitable as throwing a television out of a hotel window.

Growing vegetables had, until recently, been reserved for recovering drug addicts but there was a ground swell of enthusiasm for it. Allotments suddenly had longer waiting lists than Aston Martins.

It is quite simple and the results are very satisfying. Some things are better from the shops – roast chicken for example. It takes an enormous amount of effort to produce a roast chicken at home that is as good as one from Marks and Spencer, but with very little skill or training it's possible for one person on their own to grow much nicer vegetables than anything you can buy in the shops.

I visited as many farms as I could. I saw calves, I saw cucumbers, I saw all sorts. Organic vegetables in Aberdeenshire, a market garden at the foot of a snow-covered mountain. Broccoli, beans, kohlrabi in long pretty rows. It actually looked like a supermarket, the best supermarket I've ever seen, aisle upon aisle of neat, perfect vegetables. All I needed was a sexy trolley with big wheels and I would have got my shopping there every week.

There were weeds growing in there, attracting butterflies and bees – they all help in the end. We walked round with scissors snipping and nibbling. Vegetables picked fresh taste so good, raw. Food and sex are so close together.

I went to a whirring mechanical colossus of a farm in Down Ampney on the far side of the Cotswolds at harvest time to meet Britain's largest farmer.

It is hard to make money from agriculture. If it were easy, supermarkets would own more land than they do. Britain's biggest farmer is actually a supermarket, though: the Co-op.

Ask anyone to describe what a farmer looks like, and they'll probably start describing a man. Co-op farms are run by a woman, Christine Tachon. It's not just at the top either. The whole of farming is quite matriarchal. In small farm businesses, it's often the farmer's wife who handles the marketing and effectively calls the shots. I think women make good role models for farmers. I liked Christine. I asked her whether it was number crunching that she found most satisfying or the sight of the honeybees in the borage and then wondered if it was a stupid question. It struck me that making crops grow and making money grow are parts of the same thing. Farmers don't on the whole tend to spend much time mooning at the beauty of nature. It's poets and people from cities who do that. We went and looked at the bees. The bees were annoying, buzzing around. We had to keep our mouths shut. The borage was good, in a nice furniture kind of way, but I think you really have to be a bee to get that excited about seeing borage. Farming is a vocation, but a good farmer is not the person who gets sentimental about buttercups, but the one who can wring a high and appropriate yield from the natural buoyancy of the land. That's the drug, beating the odds. But whatever scale it was happening on, the frustrations and satisfactions were familiar.

'We're doing pumpkins for the first time this year,' said Christine, 'we're quite excited about that.'

'Actually I'm doing pumpkins for the first time this year, I'm excited about it, too,' I said.

'How many acres are you doing?'

'Well, I've got three pumpkins,' I said.

It was strange having my foot in two quite different worlds. The record industry was a sinking battleship. Even people who were quite good at their jobs were being fired or retired but the world of fine food was hiring. The prevailing mood was one of hope. The party was just getting started and the crowds were starting to arrive. Things just couldn't have been more upbeat. Selfridges were selling chickens for £60 and there was a market for them. The sky was the limit. It was apparently impossible to make food that was too good or clever and the people who were doing it were enjoying themselves more than Duran Duran did in 1984, buying yachts and marrying models.

The nation that had been the culinary laughing stock of Europe for a generation had suddenly got its act together. Our chefs were now more famous than our rock stars, and more entertaining. Rock and roll was fifty years old, and maybe there was nothing exciting left to do with it.

Things were happening fast. We'd suddenly found our taste buds, like we'd been listening to everything on crackly old 78s and someone had suddenly invented stereo. The entire menu was in a boom-like expansion phase. Heston Blumenthal opened the best restaurant in the world in London and food buyers and trend analysts from America were waiting to see what would happen here next.

Chippy has three Indian restaurants, three Chinese, and one Thai. There was a trattoria, a kebab man, two fish and chip shops, plus half a dozen solid British places. Some of them are great and none of them are dreadful, except the kebabs. There was a farmers' market in the square and in the environs there are microbreweries, cheesemakers, game dealers, farm shops, fisheries and foragers.

I like really big supermarkets, too. Big supermarkets give me goose pimples, and in Cash and Carry, the wholesalers, I'm always slightly beside myself. There is a primal thrill in the acquisition of food that even car parks, neon lights and queues for the checkout can't completely extinguish but I was about to try the real thing. I was really looking forward to going foraging. Eggy supplied all of the Michelin-starred establishments in the Cotswolds, with scavenged meats, fruits and leaves, the surprise hits of the menu, and I persuaded him to let me go with him for the day. He had a very small van and a Jack Russell that ran round in circles on my lap in the passenger seat. I explained that I only had eight hours and it was clear that he was disappointed. 'But there's just so much to see at the moment.' Eggy's passion bordered on mania and he was yammering all the way to the woods. He trained as a chef and had degrees in agriculture and in forestry but this was the only way he'd ever earned money. He constantly interrupted himself, as he pointed to things by the side of the road. 'There's wild horseradish. You need goggles to deal with that! You grate it and mix it with– Ooh, there's burdock. Makes great crisps! Bit early for that, tho– OOOh meadowsweet,' and the van screeched to a stop. Eggy had to get some meadow-sweet. We grabbed handfuls. It was a bit like elderflower but more floral and almondy, very good for ice cream, he said.

We'd parked in a forest a few minutes from Daylesford, but we might as well have arrived by spaceship. It was another world. He had a gun in the back of the van, but he pulled out a basket, for mushrooms. I carried it for him. A man can't hold a basket without looking camp. I was much happier holding a basket than a gun.

Soon Eggy found a half-eaten stump of mushroom. I thought he was going to explode. 'This will be delicious! Dee–licious,' he said, taking a long sniff. Scruffy and gnawed, it was hard to imagine it in Daylesford, or Tesco, or anywhere except a forest. It was clearly about taste not appearance.

I found the poisonous mushrooms more fascinating than the edible ones. There were a few early stinkhorns. They smell like cheese for monsters but are edible when they are young. We pulled one apart and it was a bit like a lychee inside.

Then we came across a clearing with a well-organised camp-fire. There were rough and ready benches around it, a milk churn turned into a boiler. It was easily the best restaurant I'd been to for ages. All it needed was a piano

player and it would have been perfect. We left a black toad-
stool called a King Alfred's Cake in the fireplace. Eggy said
they were good natural firelighters.

We were having fun but we still weren't doing that well,
just a few odd mushrooms to add to our half stump. 'I
picked a kilo of chanterelles in ten minutes on Monday,' he
said, hopefully.

There were a few boletuses in a larch stand, but then out
of the blue, we struck gold and what a rush of joy it was. I
began to see where his enthusiasm came from. Writing
songs, making art, doing science, anything creative is all
just foraging really. You snoop around and you don't
always know what you're looking for or where it will be or
how to recognise it and sometimes nothing happens and
then other times it's great beyond measure. We walked into
a sunny clearing and found ourselves surrounded by fairy
rings, oceans of bovine boletus, slippery jacks past count-
ing and plate-sized horse mushrooms. We filled the basket
in ten minutes. On the way home it struck me how crazy it
was that all this stuff that just grew wild commanded a
premium, was much more expensive than everything that
we grow deliberately – how little we value the mainstream
crops.

The country pubs I remember from my childhood were
about booze and crisps. They were really private members'
clubs for locals; local working men, at that. I wonder what
has become of the geezers who used to populate these

newly gentrified establishments. Rural pubs were being re-colonised. It was a grey squirrel–red squirrel situation. The lunching lady had more spending power and more friends than the solitary geezer, and slowly but surely, these women, who are not indigenous to pubs, but had escaped from kitchens all around the country, were eradicating the slightly weaker male from his habitat.

Joe Strummer once told me that after The Clash split, he'd seen The Pogues and been so rapt by their music that he joined the band more or less on the spot and spent the next couple of years touring with them. I was thinking about that when I set off to spend the evening working in the kitchen at the pub. I felt I was following my heart. There was nothing at all I'd rather have been doing. I'd become fascinated by The Plough in the village. I was eating there twice a week. Emily, the chef, had been a key player in Heston Blumenthal's team at The Fat Duck for two years. And in that time it had been voted the best restaurant in the world.

When I first met Emily, she'd just left The Fat Duck and while The Plough was being rebuilt and turned into a food laboratory, she was spending her time researching ancient local recipes and endeavouring to source all her ingredients within a few feet of the pub's front door. She came to see me about buying some lamb and we talked for ages, about brining, mainly, I think. She'd done her homework all right. She had an attention to detail that is the hallmark of genius; and madness. She was posh and pretty, her face all bones and bright eyes. It's always intriguing to meet someone who really is what they do. Comedy writers constantly crack jokes. Film people talk about films the whole time when they're not watching them. You couldn't talk to Emily for five minutes and not know that you were talking to a food luminary. She breathed it, a flood of information and ideas.

The pub, when it finally opened, lived up to all expectations and I kept asking her how she made this and how she did that, until she asked me to come and help out in the kitchen and find out for myself.

My first ever job was working in a grungy hotel kitchen, washing up for ninety pence an hour. I was no stranger to behind the scenes restaurant action. I managed to find some chefs' whites, scrubbed my fingernails and reported for duty in the late afternoon.

Emily and I sat in the sun and she talked me through the bill of fare. The bar menu of Cotswold rarebit, potted rabbit, snails, quails and real ales and then the starters, mains, cheeses and puddings from the dining room. Of course I knew it off by heart. There was a printout from Daylesford that listed all the produce currently available from their market garden. She got sidetracked when she noticed the Belles de Fontenay potatoes on their list and spent some time explaining how they make the ultimate mash.

Eggy had delivered twenty-five rabbits the previous day, which Emily had skinned, jointed and stewed for eight hours with chardonnay, lemon zest and green peppercorns but that was just the beginning.

I helped to make the potted rabbit until the rest of the team arrived at 4.30 for staff dinner. Emily went through the new items on the menu: 'Orache is like silky spinach, OK? It grows wild. It's delicious. I'll make sure you all get to taste it. The Evesham lentils are not from Evesham, but it's a traditional Evesham recipe. They used to grow lentils in Evesham two hundred years ago. Also we've got Alex's potted rabbit, OK? Saddles will be on the menu tomorrow if anyone asks. Now just a quick word about how we cook the fillet steaks. We do them *sous vide*, OK? NOT boil in the bag! The reason we cook them *sous vide*, that's vacuum wrapped, is that frying them draws all the moisture out. We poach them at a constant 65.5 °C in the temperature bath until they are uniformly medium rare all the way through, then we sear them off in a hot pan to finish them. Anyone who hasn't tasted it yet, I'll cook one for you to try later. Then you'll see how tender it is. This is not what boil in the bag is, OK? *Sous vide*. Got that?' There was much concentration and nodding of heads.

I had a whizz around the cellar. I like cellars, little under-ground sheds. There were barrels, bottles, complex mani-folds galore. They even had a Coca-Cola generator. The concentrated syrup, the elixir of cola, is the world's best hangover cure.

The Plough's kitchen was a pristine operating theatre full of excellent machines. Emily set me picking the cooked rabbit from the bones while she began to singe the hair off a piece of pork belly with a blowtorch. She was worried that the roast pork belly wasn't quite crispy enough, she'd found the answer, but I couldn't really follow the full explanation the first time around. It was a bit like the solution to Fermat's Last Theorem. Only the person who found the answer to that really understands how it works. She conducted a whole series of experiments on the spot and invented a fantastically crispy, meaty, pork belly crackler in no time. I was still administering troy weights of slow-cooked wild rabbit to a huge bowl that didn't seem to be getting any fuller.

She told me to have a rest and showed me her work-station. Each of the three chefs had their own terminal, and their own preferred tools. Emily was incredibly proud of her knives, which were frighteningly sharp: absolutely scary. The night before the pub opened, she spent three and a half hours bringing them all to a razor edge, and she tended them every day. She had a whole range of spoons, acidulated water for cleaning, cooking salt, a selection of big bowls, plenty of paper towels. All her food ingredients were well organised in a chiller cabinet below the work surface.

It was all brilliantly organised and free from clutter. Emily's day started at 7 a.m. and it hadn't stopped. The food is all prepared during the day, and during service it is mainly a question of just finishing the cooking. The chips for example have already been cooked twice, once in water, once in a mixture of goose fat and rapeseed oil, and now they just needed finishing in very hot oil. The Scotch duck's eggs had already been crumbed and pannéd and just needed a quick whirl in the goosefat fryer.

The huge extractor fan over the range was glugging away and the temperature in the kitchen was pretty comfortable. 'The fridge blew up yesterday!' said Emily. 'Nightmare!' She showed me the drystore, full of great sacks of flour and lentils. The pot-washer arrived, and the other two chefs; we were all at our stations ready for action by 5.45 p.m. I continued with my rabbit picking. Emily tasted the meat. She tasted and tested everything. She added more pepper and parsley, then some lemon juice, showed me how to fudge the meat into a ramekin and went to clarify some butter on the range. I'd made a scant couple of dozen potted rabbits out of all that cooking and preparation and potted rabbit was a minor feature of the bar snack menu. Emily poured on the clarified butter and whipped the ramekins into the blast chiller; a very satisfying freezer that billowed large amounts of ice vapour into the room every time it was opened. It was very theatrical: a rock fridge. She mainly used it to cool stocks very quickly to fridge temperature so they wouldn't go bad.

Then the first order came through from the dining room. Orders came through to the kitchen on a printout like an old-fashioned telex machine and the time the order came through is written on a whiteboard. The first one was slightly disappointing. Two ladies, one wanted halibut and one wanted chocolate pudding. Emily shouted out the order to a chorus of yeses from her sous chefs. The next order was also a bit of a damp squib: two chips and a side salad. There were forty-two covers booked, plus there would be walk up. It was eight o'clock and all we'd had so far was four half orders. 'We're going to get smashed in a minute!' said Emily. 'Smashed to bits!' There was nothing to do but wait. The atmosphere was just like backstage at a gig before going on to a packed house. I watched the meringue machine whirr. It was calming, mesmerising and I floated off into my thoughts. Suddenly all the bread had disappeared and the front of house staff were yelling for more butterballs like there was a fire that could only be extinguished by butterball. We were off, under Emily's supreme command as she deftly managed the limited resources. 'Don't be a hero Simon! Get Alex to help. Alex, three artichokes and a side salad from the walk-in fridge please,' she sang, whilst rescuing a liver pâté and deep-frying a duck egg and studying the next order – 'One rabbit!' (cheers all round the kitchen for my first order). One rabbit, one rarebit, one omelette. I put a rarebit in the oven and watched Simon whisk an egg white to a foam in seconds flat and stir in the yolk with butter. It was a soufflé. It looked delicious, so hypnotically delicious I nearly burnt the toast for the rarebit. It was like being in a cavalry charge. I didn't know which way to look, but I knew I was fighting for the true and just cause.

The finished dishes arrived at the plate warmer, which lit them up like balls on a snooker table. It was like looking at a photograph. Emily checked everything before it left the kitchen. There was so much happening, butter emulsions bubbling away, grill permanently on full blast, a pot wash-ing frenzy. It was like being on stage: live, live, live. The waitresses keeping us posted on what was happening on the other side of the door: 'It's amazing out there, really good atmosphere. They're loving it.' 'Can we get table eighteen's starters? They are complaining!' 'They love the steak on table seven!' Emily had sold eighty-six steaks in five days. Word had got around the village that they are rather special. 'Who's reducing water here?' she cried, exasperated at a pot bubbling on the range.

The blowtorch was out again and a baked Alaska flew out of the door. Poached nectarines, chocolate doughnuts followed.

I learned more tricks that night than I ever have on a cookery course. I thought about working there every week to find out how they make everything. It's hard work, but making stuff, especially food, made me feel very good indeed. I always thought music was a universal language, but it is actually a tribal one, an exclusive dialect. Food is the most basic and shareable human pleasure. It unites everybody: the young, the old, any culture, any creed. Food is the music of love.

CHAPTER 9

LOVE

I'd come to love all the heaps. The essence of life on a farm, monuments of the recyclable, heaps are almost alive. It was like getting a new pet, getting a new pile – maybe not a dog or pig class of creature, but definitely something at the tortoise or goldfish level of commitment. There were many around the farm, some were getting smaller, some were growing. A heap can never stay the same, it's an evolving process. My favourite pile, the crushed concrete cone, was shrinking fast. It got used for various things, filling up holes, tracks, sub-floors: all sorts. It had always looked like a huge pile of crushed concrete, but suddenly in the spring all kinds of sprouting savannah-style greenery started emerging. I wasn't ready for that: a reaction without an action. It was life affirming, all these robust, vigorous shoots growing out from nothing but crushed-up concrete. It was the exact opposite of the Chelsea Flower Show, which I also loved but was so meticulously planned and tidy. It would have appalled the judges, that concrete mountain weed garden, but I loved it.

One of the main things that living on a farm taught me was to accept chaos and not to panic when it looked untidy. In London piles of stuff can't just sit around. Everything has to have an immediate purpose. Space is too valuable for anything that's not being used. Out here it was cheaper to leave things lying around than to move them.

The east face of the concrete was sheer and unconquerable, but I managed the north-western ascent. It is a great thing to be able to look down on where you live. Altitude is a drug. It was perfectly still and almost magic that evening, just warm enough and clear skies forever.

Down on the ground, the huge mound of manure from the excavated slurry pit, twenty-five years' worth, was a seething mass of thistles and nettles. It was like it was on fire, a raging bio mess. It was a good fertiliser, under the nettles. If I didn't know what it was I would never have known there was a heap there at all now. It just looked like a jungle. It was the richest, freshest, best soil but it was attracting the most ordinary, invasive species. The prettiest flowers were growing out of the random rubble pile from a couple of big farm sheds I'd taken down a few months before. There were poppies there and forget-me-nots.

Some problems took a long time to solve. Hedges needed constant attention; the farm had miles of hedges because the meadows were quite small. Even the garden hedges were a handful. There was an overgrown beech hedge in the back garden that took three years to repair. It actually looked more like a wood than a hedge to start with, but Daphne was sure it was a hedge. The magic moment came when a team of three men came to take the straggly top off and a perfectly formed baby hedge emerged from the jumble. My patience was always rewarded in the end but my, oh my, what a fiddle.

It paid to be steady but bold. It's amazing how much one man can do in one week with a really big digger. I'd always liked the spot down by the railway line. I had just left it to do its thing since we'd got here, but that chunk of land – an acre or two – hadn't been farmed for generations. Previous owners had buried their favourite horses down there, hidden asbestos, things like that, but over the last couple of years it had become completely impassable and I thought I'd send the digger in there for a week and see what we ended up with.

The sun was warm on my face and drew me into the outside. I couldn't help myself. I was overwhelmed by long forgotten feelings: the unexpected kiss of clemency and a proper sense of spring. Before I knew what I was doing, I was on my way down there to see what the digger was up to. The heron rose off the pond and skirted the woods, low. I spotted a fox, too. It had been so long since I'd seen one it made me shiver as I caught sight of it, darting down the hedge line. So sinuous against the plonky sheep. It was muddy from the caterpillar tracks and I'd ruined my last decent pair of shoes.

All the undergrowth had already been removed and there were just a few handsome specimen trees left, a couple of huge ancient oaks and down by the railway line, one that had fallen. It was so massive it would have taken three people holding hands to ring the trunk. It must have been lying there for years but would have been worth a fortune as timber and I was amazed no one had chopped it all up and sold it for cash. I'd been fiddling around with drawings for climbing frames for weeks but that fallen tree was better than anything I could have dreamed up. The kids still love it. I sat down on it for the first time and discovered it was home to a hundred kinds of creepy crawlies. Ditches that had long sat stagnant, were gurgling and bubbling and, where there had been a bog, there was a lake with the bare mound of an island in the middle. I couldn't wait for the ducks to move in. In the past the island had been home to dozens. I'd been told it was the best duck shoot in the area. The water acts as a moat that keeps the foxes out. There was a secret underwater path to the island, so it was just about possible to walk to it in wellies, but Paddy said if I went that way I had to make sure there were no foxes looking.

It's the only way to clear up really, with an excavator. Having a digger around didn't cost that much more than sitting in a taxi. I kept it on, and did a bit more tidying up. No one had had a good go at the yard for decades and after just one day the place was hardly recognisable.

Suddenly, we were living in a world of bright colours again: a bonanza of bud and blossom; massed dandelions and clumps of bluebells punching through the reinvigorated greens like exclamation marks. There were daisies everywhere, the small ordinary ones. The big leggy oxeyes come later when the grass in the corners is waist deep. Properly, daisies probably shouldn't have been there. Like so many of the best things about the countryside, they weren't part of any design either. It was just that we had four lawnmowers, not one of which quite worked.

Once you have a couple of lawnmowers, they start to multiply. If people see a shed with lawnmowers and bits of lawnmowers in it, they start to bring you their lawnmowers and the situation gets worse. 'It's practically perfect. Just needs a couple of blades replacing. My mate gave it to me for nothing, so you can have it if you like.' Like some kinds of insect many lawnmowers die at the end of summer and I think it's hard for a man to throw out anything with an engine that still works.

What no one seemed to realise is that lawnmower engines never, ever break. That's why they use them on Microlight aircraft. It's always the whirly bits that go wrong with these things, not the engine. One lawnmower needed that bit, so one of Blackham's gang had helpfully brought along another that had the right bit intact. That particular bit didn't quite fit where it was supposed to, but someone always had another lawnmower that might be good for parts for the one that had just arrived. I was surrounded by a daisy chain of lawnmowers that did everything except mow lawns.

There is nothing like lawn. Everyone loves springing around barefoot on the grass when everything looks pretty in the sunshine, but I began to appreciate shades of grey as well. Flowers don't really start performing until the sky darkens. Sometimes, just after it had rained, it was like all the petals had been switched on. I started to find those glistening grey moments and their fanfare of glowing blooms more heartening than a conventional sunny day.

Small children prefer the bright simplicity of the sunshine. All children find daisies fascinating and pick and present them to anyone who will pay attention. The scale of a daisy is perfect for a tiny thumb and finger, and the flower speaks a bright language of perfect symmetry and colour to anyone who will listen. So I found myself looking hard at the simple, understated perfection of the daisy for a second time and enjoying it with perhaps more wonder and mystification than I did before I learned how to speak. God bless the daisy. More English than the rose, and just as beautiful.

As I studied the daisies, it occurred to me how many different kinds of bees there seemed to be, now I'd started to notice them, and I found myself falling into that bottomless well of intrigue and fascination, the feast of exquisite detail that is the nirvana of the quiet country gentleman, at least one who's not too bothered about mowing the lawn. Beauty passes unnoticed and forgotten so easily.

Rural nirvana is a vegetative state. There's nowhere finer than the countryside for being bone idle and that's because there are always a hundred little things that really need taking care of: roses need pruning, tractor needs tuning, leaks need patching, mice need catching. Once there are a few things that need to be done, it is pleasant enough to sit around not doing any of them. It's hard for television to capture the greatest aspects of the countryside. It all looks pretty enough, but peace and quiet don't broadcast particularly well, however good they feel. Suddenly everything was green, especially the lake which was almost iridescent. It had never been quite right, that lake, but it'd never been this particular shade before. The Canada geese that had been living there sloped off in disgust. I found one of them in the next field, sulking. It was peaceful, a display of orchids in the wood and the cuckoo stating the minor third, ducks sitting on watercress, the dog quietly gnawing on a rabbit. I wondered if I'd ever get bored of the place. I didn't think so. Its pleasures were infinite.

Blackham and co. had got it looking quite cosy in the static caravan. Paddy bought it for nine hundred quid just after we moved in and the price was still painted on one of the windows. I liked it in there, though. So did the gang. They all had their own spots and mugs. The garden master plan seemed to have its own seat, as well. It had become a member of the family, too. Earlier in the year, when the new garden was still a field, the drawing had to be stuck back together after the dog got hold of it, and nowadays it looked like a treasure map, covered in muddy thumb-prints, coffee cup rings, quite a lot of 'X's marking spots and mystic annotations. It was briefly believed to have been lost the previous week, but Claire had it. Blackham took it home and spent the weekend with it trying to make sure the electricity and water supplies didn't have to cross or share ditches – a complex problem of higher mathematics similar to the 'Bridges of Königsberg', which has no solu-tions in three dimensions. After mulling it over with the plant hire catalogue he reckoned the conundrum, which he had been approaching with a backhoe loader, was only solvable with a three-tonne dumper and a mini excavator. When they arrived on a low loader it was more exciting than hiring a Ferrari or getting picked up in a helicopter.

I didn't expect building a garden to be as interesting as sitting in one doing nothing, but when it was all done I wasn't sure whether the finished thing was as much fun as the work in progress. Building things is better than things themselves. Things just sit there, finished, over and boring by comparison. Part of me wanted to keep digging and dumping forever. There was all kinds of stuff coming out of the ground, clay tiles and engineering bricks, under-ground springs and keystones. It must have been beautiful before, maybe a hundred years ago. For some months now, the area had looked just like a battlefield. Visitors gasped at the jeopardy of what used to be a fairly passable meadow with a half-arsed Stonehenge in the middle. It was now stripped back to bare its bottom, and riven with Blackham's trench matrices filling slowly with ground water. It looked dramatic but how wrong can a garden go, really? It can't. Any kind of action in a garden has a positive effect. It would be hard to get a garden wrong, or do it in bad taste. If all else failed there was nothing that couldn't be solved with a bigger digger. 'Excavate et Rexcavate' became my new motto. It applies to everything, not just gardening.

But gardens take a lot of understanding and coming to terms with, too. There came a point when it dawned on me that finally, after years of making mistakes, I was getting to grips with how buildings worked. I finally managed to locate and fix a leak that had been puzzling me since we moved in. Water was entering the building near the satellite dish, via an old chimney I had no idea existed. The television hadn't worked since the leak was fixed but you can't have everything. Buildings are quite simple, but gardens are really complex by comparison. They're alive for starters. Everyone said swimming pools were the worst, the thing most likely to drive a man insane, but I must say gardens were pretty exasperating. The rose garden was under reconsideration. When I originally planted it, the rabbits ate most of it. The remains of it lay underwater. I had to start again, I pulled everything out, put in a new drain and installed an electric fence. I refused to be beaten. Strange how the oasis of peace and harmony I dreamed of was a war raging in a disaster zone.

*   *   *

Now there were bees turning up everywhere: in cupboards, in curtains, in clusters. A swarm had landed on the roof while I was away and they were very much at home in the eaves by the time I got back. We were on our way to pick the kids up from school one Monday and a bee that had got in the car stung Claire on her finger. She clearly thought she was going to die. From then on she just went very quiet whenever bees came near. Something had to be done. Paddy said I should call Viktor. 'He's all about bees,' he said. Viktor said he'd be there as soon as he could. There was a pair of bare athletic legs in the window, half way up a ladder the next time I came in to make coffee. A small crowd of nannies and cleaners had gathered to watch.

Out in the back garden an incredibly handsome man wearing only shorts and a T-shirt was digging around in the timbers puffing one of those smoky things at a very excited mass of bees. 'I trry to ketch quee–un,' he said, with a grin and a heavy Russian accent. 'Don't you need a spacesuit?' I said. 'Yus, I haff. Iss no problem,' he said, pulling out a small piece of honeycomb and brushing some bees off his smile. I went back in to make him some coffee and the girls didn't even seem to see me. An hour later he was still out there and they were still finding things to do in the kitchen. Only thing to do was take the roof off, he said, or kill them. I could tell he wanted to take the roof off. 'How do we kill them?' I asked. 'I don't know,' he said, 'I never kill bee. I like bee.' That was fairly obvious. They seemed to like him, too. We talked it over. They had to go, no way round it and he said he'd do it. We thought maybe we'd set up some hives a bit further from the house, which pleased him immensely. He said he'd come back the next week with all the bits and pieces.

The story goes that the cleverer you are, the more interesting you find bees. There was an Oxford don nearby, a professor, who had millions. He was gone, daddy, gone, off with the bees: watching them dance and staring at their honey, stupefied. Like higher mathematics, once you've really tasted bees, they can run away with you and there may be no going back. Maybe that's why, although they were always quite near the top of my shopping list, I still hadn't started a hive. People who live on farms all tend to be quite passionate about what they keep. They usually want to share their joy, and that, combined with the charm of the animals, can be hard to resist. Despite all my misgivings, I had still very nearly bought a herd of Ayrshire cows just the previous week while under the enchantment of a dairyman. Come to think of it, I'd only bought the pigs by accident. So, whenever I went to meet a farmer and his closest friends, I went very cautiously.

An apple is a triumph of natural design, beauty all the way. The more times I saw a tree bearing a full crop of apples, the more enchanting I found it. Apples are so practical. They last for ages if laid out in a shed. The autumn crop would still eat well, right into spring. Some of them even tasted better after a couple of months as the flavours developed. The apple trees I'd planted the previous year were already bearing fruit, but I still wasn't sure what mulberry trees looked like and I'd been growing one for four years. I'd bought a mulberry shortly after we moved in for fifty quid. Yew trees are famous in the realms of things that happen slowly, but the row of two pound fifty yews I had planted at the same time, were really going some; as bushy as a bear's eyebrows. The mulberry looked exactly, exactly the same as it did when it arrived: a stick. I was determined to have mulberries. The glamour of the mulberry had grown with every passing year to the point where it was now irresistible. I still hadn't seen an actual mulberry. I wondered what they looked like in real life. I wondered what they smelled like. I thought about what taste this, the most English of all fruits, might have, and it tantalised me. I re-entered the mulberry tree market at the four hundred pound level and a *Morus nigra* arrived by overnight delivery from Holland. Daphne's clients were all terribly impatient, bad-tempered and rich. Not the sort of people who had time to wait for their mulberries to grow. Daffers was always getting container loads of forest canopy shipped over from Holland. She phoned me a couple of times to warn me it was coming and what to do with it when it got here and all the rest of it. The delivery guy was a panicker. He was not equipped to deal with express deliveries and slow-growing plants. He broke everyone with his anxieties. I was having a rest when he arrived.

I love a nap in the afternoon. I love a nap in the afternoon possibly more than I have ever loved anything: much more than mulberry trees. Claire woke me up to tell me the tree guy was here, like the fire brigade had turned up. He didn't know what to do with it. She didn't know what to do with him. 'Look he's a tree guy, with a lorry full of trees. What's the problem? How big is it? Can we move it with the digger?' I was starting to think the thing must be absolutely massive. A picture formed in my mind. 'Just tell him to dump it. I'll get a crane in, the kids'll love that.' I was sure it could sit there another hour. I was pretty certain it wouldn't do much in an hour. Then the au pair came up in tears saying 'man in big lorry let chickens out'. Then the lorry blocked the drive and Crudgie couldn't get home so I had to wade in. Outside, the chickens, cheese man and tree man had all disappeared and there standing in a tub in the middle of the drive was a mulberry twig exactly the same as the one I'd already got. I lifted it out of the way. It wasn't as tall as any of the apple trees. I could have had another whole orchard if I'd spent the money on apple and pear trees. I suppose there's not as much demand for mulberries. I'm still not sure what they look like.

The first lettuces were coming out of the converted tomato shed-greenhouse (the greenshed) already. That shed was gigantic, I had wondered if I was being excessive when I built it but it was instantly clear that glasshouses, like sock drawers and suitcases, are never quite big enough. Always bulging at the seams. Most of the greenshed was being colonised by a giant melon beanstalk. It grew at an alarming rate. It was hard to say if it was a bush or a tree or what it would do next. It grew and grew until almost the entire shed, which had once housed dozens of battery beef calves, was supporting an organism bearing a single precious melon just big enough for a snack for one person.

'I'm going to look at the dandelions,' I said. 'There's loads of them.'

Back when we got married, I was in a famous band. You can never be sure why people like you when you're success-ful or famous. Well, actually, I suppose you can. I don't know what she was expecting: more than dandelions? Perhaps.

'I'll come,' she said.

'Come on. Hurry up, then. It's happy hour.'

It was the end of the day and suddenly still and sunny. Our star was taking its final curtain call of the day. Earlier there had been hail so heavy you had to raise your voice against it, wind hard from all quarters and rolling thunder, with skies so grey and groany all might have seemed hope-less to anyone who hadn't spotted the pink flowers by the pond. But now, gold light was flying in sideways, and green and blue were everywhere and looked good together for spring. Sometimes in that hour before sunset, the light is so rich and dazzling that even a green pile of tyres sitting on a concrete slab looks like God might have put them there just to show off.

It was all so pretty it seemed completely abstract, suddenly, but there were practicalities to consider too. I had to break into the shed where the quad was. I was wrenching the door open with very little refinement, when she arrived, with her hood pulled tight around her head and her hands jammed into her middle.

I wasn't sure whether to be angry with Blackie for locking the quad up and going home with the key, or for not locking it up properly, as I was inside in twenty seconds. She kicked stones while I fiddled about trying to make it start and she laughed when I graunched the wall reversing out. She hung on, her chin resting on my shoulder, face peeping out of the hood and her curves pushing into my back. The dog came, too. We zoomed up the dirt track in tandem towards the top field where I'd seen the dandelions the day before. A couple of roe deer had bounced off into the woods and the pair of geese took flight on sight of the whirring whippet. They began their take-off roll as we arrived at full tilt. He peeled away towards them and then we were following him. I know he will chew my favourite guitar one day, he's already started on the piano legs, but there is nothing to compare to a whippet on the bound – they can accelerate faster than a leopard. There was a lot of grace to spare in that chase. The huge birds gliding in ground effect, the dog, easily faster, racing low, hugging at the ground with each step, just playing with them.

The thunderstorms had washed away the haze and given the big sponge a drink. Six kinds of weather in one day, a mad spin cycle. A tree that had buds on clearly definable branches the night before, looked green and fuzzy on top that evening. Perfectly sculpted anvils of cumulonimbus spotted the horizon. There was a glimpse of a stately home through the trees. We were zooming through an immaculate stationary eternity, a landscape arrested by sunshine, at sixty miles an hour. Sheep were statuesque on the mound. Some of the hedgerows were pure white with blossom, others still asleep. It was all so colourful.

'It's nice,' she said, 'I didn't know you could come this way.'

We stopped in the middle of the huge field at the centre of a pristine green landscape on the very threshold of spring. The sun warm on our faces and the engine warm on our behinds.

'What are those clouds called?'

'Cumulonimbus,' I said. 'CBs.'

'They're incredibly violent.'

But they looked like decorations on a Christmas tree.

Then the engine died.

'There's no fuel,' she said, 'I told you.'

'There's loads of fuel. It's just a lemon, this thing.'

I couldn't make it start so she started back towards the house with the dog, on foot. I passed her five minutes later in the middle of the dandelions.

'I can't slow down or it'll stop, do you want to hop on?' I hollered.

She was shaking her head and smiling and in her hand was a little bunch of dandelions.

*　　*　　*

I was having a stare with Fred, the next afternoon. There is a gate at the bottom of the barn and he leans on it looking out across the valley. There was mist in the valley and sun was streaming into the barn and the new lambs were standing in the patches of light. It all looked like a corny greetings card. 'One of them tups has had it!' said Fred, nodding at a dead ram in the corner. I hadn't noticed it. It was one of seven or eight that services what must be a couple of thousand ewes. I said, 'Seven rams take care of the whole lot of them!?' He said, 'Ah, they never bloody last long.'

'You know,' I said to Claire, 'a good rule of thumb for birthday parties is only to invite people who you know well enough to fart in front of. Take intimacy over extravagance,' I implored, 'you'll have a much nicer time.' But it was, as she pointed out, her birthday, not mine and she wanted to raise the roof. So, we threw open all the doors and made merry on a large scale. The piano player fell through. I undercooked the venison. During the fireworks I noticed a sozzled, grinning billionaire, swaying like a peculiar sunflower in a bed of miniature ferns that I'd been carefully nurturing for a year or more, but none of that seemed to matter. There were greater forces at work. It was fantastic. As I lit the bonfire early on, the smoke rose away perpendicular, not a breath of wind anywhere. It was an extraordinarily calm and clear evening, perhaps the first one of the summer, a little pause. The house was full of life, all the lights were on, all the fires were roaring as the night drew on and music and laughter ached from every corner. Perhaps parties are only that good once in a lifetime.

I was wandering round the house and garden alone at about 4 a.m., still glowing with the glamour of it all, quietly singing Leadbelly's 'Rock Island Line' to myself as I turned out lights, and blew out candles – there was definitely at least one of those that would have started a fire if I hadn't spotted it. I was just congratulating myself on that, when I heard the noise. It was an impossible sound to ignore: insistent, vulnerable, charming. 'Peep, peep, peep, peep,' it went. 'Peeeep. Peeeeeeep!' It was a chicken. A newborn chicken. About a month before, we'd bought an incubator on the internet. There was all kinds of chicken paraphernalia available: little hospitals for sick chicks with oxygen tents and defibrillators. I went for the smallest incubator, a tiny one, one that held three eggs. As soon as it arrived the next three eggs that were laid went straight in there and the thing had been a source of fascination to all ever since. The au pair was the undisputed authority on eggs and chicks. She had hatched duck eggs, goose eggs, all sorts, in a domestic incubator back home in Bulgaria. 'What will happen?' the children had been asking her every day for a month, always keen to hear it all over again, their fascination insatiable.

Well, whatever was going to happen had happened, and there was no question that the thing could stay where it was. The egg phase of its cycle was in the past now and it was ready to move on right away. It was making that very clear. I took the cover off the incubator and pulled the thing out of the remains of its shell. 'Peep. Peep. Peep.' Wriggle. Well a birthday party was one thing, but this was a greater species of event, a birth, just a tiny one, but this most humble of creatures, probably the most abused, under-valued, downtrodden animal on the planet, so alive, alert and cute in my hand. Miraculous. It was enough to make me gasp and send me into open-mouthed wonder, almost bring a tear to my tired eye. It would have melted the cold-est of hearts. 'Peep.' Wriggle. Steps needed to be taken, immediately. That was for sure. I couldn't wake the au pair. Out of the question. I would have to deal with it. I wished I'd listened more carefully to what she'd been telling the children. I went to the chicken coop and put it in a little nest of hay with its fellow creatures while I tried to work out a plan. It was obviously too cold in there, but I didn't want the thing thinking I was its mummy. I'm sure she'd said something about that. It was peeping its little head off and the big chickens weren't doing anything so I took it back in my hand and woke Claire. 'Peep,' it said. 'There's a little box on the shelf with hay in it. Put it in there,' she said. I gave it a little saucer of water with some bread in and set the whole thing next to the fire and got into bed and watched her sleeping. I still didn't know why she loved me. She told me once that I had a good nose. And she thinks it's funny when I dribble. That's a really good sign.

* * *

My sister got married. I guess she married 'up'. Her father-in-law collected paintings by Canaletto. My father collected things like outboard engines and coils of rope. Mind you, my mother did once have her bottom squeezed by Damien Hirst. They were going to get married down here on the farm, but as I suspected, it might have worked out much cheaper to have the wedding in Sloane Square and the reception in Mayfair. There was a bishop and everything: still miles cheaper. I liked that bishop. He had the best outfit of everybody. He completely understood showbusiness and set the fastest time of the day for a namedrop from a standing start. Actually no one could compete with him. His trump card was that he actually knew God quite well, and kind of made me wish I did too. He said he'd noticed people always cry more at weddings than at funerals. I had been completely overcome when my sister appeared. That's the best moment of the day, when the whole sea of hats turns smiling to catch a glimpse of the bride.

I spent most of the service gawping at my own wife, who had been stumbling around in baggy pyjamas, dealing with babies for almost as long as I could remember. Suddenly, there she was wearing a red dress, hat and heels and immaculate in her rediscovered beauty. I swear she was six-feet-two in those shoes. It was the first time I'd heard the wedding vows since we got married. They seemed to make even more sense years after we said them than they did in the passion of romance.

What had started out as a kind of madness between us had become quite a sensible business by now, a bit what

55

like happens with a successful rock and roll band. There's always something that's a bit out of control about being in love and I'm still never sure what's going to happen next. Moving to the farm, removing ourselves from everything we'd known, was the most romantic thing we could possibly have done. We'd done some spectacular things together, but you can do spectacular things with anybody and have a great time. I suppose love is when you're happy to do nothing together. I think the best thing about marriage is the intimacy of quiet moments. Love is as simple as when you've made two cups of tea, giving the other person the cup that looks the nicer colour.

I suppose in order to fall in love we had to be born around the same time and then we had to be in the same place, once. These things were beyond control. We could so easily never have met. I remember the moment I knew I wanted to marry Claire very clearly. I suddenly realised I wanted to have children: her children, and I'd never felt like that. Maybe children were the reason for getting married, but they changed everything as well.

We were pretty shellshocked by the first, but just before the twins were born I remember saying, 'Better take a deep breath. As soon as they arrive, we're on the rollercoaster and we're not going to be able to remember what this was like.' And I really can't remember. I think we used to have breakfast in bed. Children come with all this forward momentum. Suddenly we were on a journey and one of us was holding the map and the other one was driving, and the one who's driving always thinks it was the turn back there, and the one with the map doesn't like the way the other one is doing things.

We are always arguing about something. The day we stop arguing is the day it's over. As the vicar who married us said, 'Forget about "me", it's "we" from now on' and that's about the size of it.

SUMMER

CHAPTER 10

FAMILY AND FRIENDS

Blackie's son finished school and started coming to work with his dad. He was in Blackham's band as well. Lead guitar. Blackie was showing him around and he had some questions for me, mainly about guitars, which I did my best to swerve. Then the gardener was wondering about bay trees and wanted me to look at them with her. The cleaners arrived and said that there were sheep in the road. Charlie, the fence and digger man, showed up just in time, and once we'd all caught the sheep, there wasn't enough time to talk about field gates because I had to go to Cirencester. There was never quite time to talk to Charlie about field gates. There was never time to deal with the gates. Every single one on the farm was an antique and none of them swung properly.

*   *   *

I didn't want to be late for my appointment in the capital of the Cotswolds. I was due to meet the farmer and the cows at Highgrove to have a look at the royal milk, with a view to making some seriously posh cheese. I drove through the late morning and hobbity hills and dragony dales in streaming sunshine with a rare sense of bliss. I was so accustomed to the farm now that even the next valley seemed a foreign place where the grass was a different shade of green. The Prince of Wales is a cheese man. He had spent decades assembling what turned out to be the most beautiful herd of cows I'd ever seen. A lot of care and thought had gone into those Ayrshire cows. The rare breed, the housing, what they ate. It was perfect in every detail. I plunged my hand into the silage they were munching on and pulled out a plug. It was intoxicating, full of delicate chemistry. I stood there glugging on it like a fat cigar until I felt dizzy.

It was always good to see other farms. There was something particularly reassuring about seeing the prince's devotion to this one. There was a time when people lampooned him for his views on organic farming. There were times when I thought I might have lost the plot, asked myself what the hell I was doing. I'd just been following a whim, born out of falling in love, but it was good to know I was keeping such illustrious company. I hadn't really considered it. It wasn't just royalty: now I considered it, in the pleasant fug of another big sniff of cow's breakfast in the future king's garden. Every billionaire going seemed to be enjoying a kind of second life of some kind, a happy ever after phase. I'd met the Kindersleys, of the Dorling Kindersley publishing house, at a flower show. They had sold up and shipped out, and were now running an organic farm and making nice-smelling herbal remedies. Both husband and wife were full of the joys of chickens and pigs. There was so much to say. Pig owners are all long lost friends. We were talking about whether it was best to artificially inseminate or not, until the tea ran out. '*Such* a shame,' said Peter Kindersley, because I'd apparently only just missed the man who used to run Bradford and Bingley. He was now a cheesemaker of some repute and had been forced to rush off on some urgent business, which is the way it is with cheesemakers.

It must happen quite often that people think they're settling down to a quiet life and discover passions they didn't know they had and end up becoming so absorbed and involved in what they do, they end up working harder than they did before they stopped working.

The world of celebrity, the endless treadmill of red carpet, had become a much more closely scrutinised environment than it had been. Fame had once been quite liberating, a badge of freedom. Now it could be suffocating. There was more and more media, and less and less happening. Celebrity was a much more carefully husbanded and traded resource than it had been. Even without the frisson of an encounter with the royal cows I had all the glamour I needed. It was a quiet world, but fascinating. I'd almost forgotten that moving to the country had ever been a gamble. A farm is something to do, as well as somewhere to be. A manor house or a rectory might have been the standard rock star purchases of choice, but the farm sputtering back to life was the reason it was all turning out all right for me. When I stopped pushing, it pulled me along with it. It was impossible not to get swept along in the bounty, buoyancy, the continuous currents of nature. It still seemed ridiculous that an actual chunk of England, something this endless and wonderful could even have an owner. It was like owning the sea or the stars. Of course you don't have to own it to enjoy it. The English countryside is a vast, dilapidated stately home that is open to everybody. Fields in Europe and North America are different things from English meadows. They are huge, planned on the scale of the gigantic machines that cultivate them, not for people. They make an unappealing habitat. England's green and pleasant land is totally impractical for agricultural purposes and hugely expensive to run, but the whole thing is a kind of Grade I listed national monument and a wonderful place to live.

It didn't suit everybody. Two or three of the local trophy mansions kept on changing hands. There was a couple living in an utterly fabulous house nearby. It had an indoor swimming pool, a Bentley on the gravel and a cinema in the cellar, but the wife told me she felt she had nothing to do. She found herself isolated, unhappy and eventually became seriously depressed. For some people the country was suffocating.

It was just what I'd needed, particularly the garden. We grew together. If I wasn't there I was thinking about it or trying to get there. It had completely replaced the pub as my place of sanctuary. There was much to be said for fiddling around in the parish at large, but I was happiest in my own garden with my family around me. Even if I went out for the day I would find myself missing it and wondering what was going on. If I was in the farm office, I'd keep having to take a peek if it started raining, or if the sun came out, or if it was cloudy. Any excuse to see what the artichokes were doing.

We took the kids to Bournemouth and so much had happened while we were away I was devastated. The more time I spent in the garden, the more compelling it was. Leaving it became quite a wrench.

When I got back from Cirencester – I hadn't even left the Cotswolds – I found nineteen ducks had arrived on the lake, not the duck pond, but at least it was a start. Nature's seal of approval was a resounding triumph. I'd fought with that lake. It had been misbehaving since we got here, mainly because it was fed by every ditch and drain on the farm and in order for it to work, they all needed to work. It had been leaking and going green on a regular basis. It had finally settled down a bit to the point where I was beginning to think it might be safe to buy some ducks, but they'd happened all by themselves.

I asked Blackie about putting some trout in there and he said it was full of trout and tench and barbel. They'd swum up from the river. I was so proud I put a flagpole up in the yard.

* * *

Builders materialise in old houses like ducks on open water. I was completely addicted to building. I couldn't stop. Bathrooms, kitchens and bedrooms, stuff that was a prerequisite for living was one thing, but having the resources to build, on a more casual basis, just because I wanted to was much more fun. There were lots of building materials on site because we'd taken down so many old buildings by now. Having materials around was like an alcoholic having some beer in the fridge. I couldn't just let them sit there. Telegraph poles were the worst. There is almost nothing you can't build out of telegraph poles. There was a derelict farmhouse up for auction just around the corner and several times I caught myself dreaming of that house, of selling the restored farm and buying the derelict one just so I could rebuild it.

Claire and I had been so wrapped up in each other I hadn't given a thought to the people we might meet when we moved to the country. I thought we'd be keeping the world at arm's length, that we'd be alone living quietly, having escaped from other people altogether. I don't suppose I'd really considered it. It is hard to be alone. The bigger and more complicated a house is, and the higher the fence that goes around it, the harder it is to lock the world outside. Privacy is a modern notion, really. The farm always had been a little community of its own. The cast was still expanding. Now there was a bookkeeper in the office, as well as the builders, the farm hands and the gardener, not to mention all the beetles, birds, badgers and bats that the place was home to. It was a zoo. The nanny's brother moved in, and then the landlady from the pub. The house was full to the rafters with people, dogs, apples and children. I counted, as I left the house one morning, eleven cars sitting in the yard and I could only identify the owners of seven of them. I hadn't seen a rat for a while, thanks to the two extra dogs, one very large, one very small – but there was an outbreak of headlice. There was also at least one verruca at large, and certain members of the household were carrying a peculiar, faintly medieval skin condition called hand, foot and mouth. It was utter chaos.

The house had become so busy. I spent all day in my shed where it was quiet. I think it only gets worse, the more stuff you have. People who live in huge stately homes have to allow the public into their bedrooms on Thursdays, and famous people just don't stand a chance. When I'd last visited Miami, I went for a whizz on a Microlight seaplane. The pilot said, 'Do you want to see Madonna's house?' I said, 'Not really.' He took off and flew straight to it, circled around it, very low and loud. 'It's Madonna's house,' he said. I said, 'She doesn't live here any more.' He said, 'Yeah, it's her old house.' No wonder she scarpered. I quite liked having all these people around, though. I just didn't think I was coming to a party when I moved to the country. I thought I was leaving one.

There were so many calls on my attention, so much drama, so many ways to potter around blissfully. 'But what do you do in the evenings?' 'What are the cool pubs?' my old friends would say – and it was quite hard to explain. 'Well, sometimes when the moon is up we go out in the garden, but we don't really, er, do anything, much.' It's not really a place, it's more of a feeling than anything. It's hard to explain the joys of wellington boots and strap-on torches to people who are looking for excitement.

It doesn't take much to turn heads and get tongues wagging in the country. I knew Claire's old friend Camilla had arrived because Blackie, who was mowing the lawn, came to tell me there was an 'Evo 8' parked outside. 'Top of the range!' he said with a big smile. Don't forget he used to play drums in Hawkwind, and had seen all kinds of far-out freaky stuff, but the car, which was the third fastest on the road, had set off an electrical storm in his brain. Camilla was rather beautiful and was wearing a short skirt, which all added to the impact. Her arrival brought everything to a standstill, like the Red Arrows flying overhead unexpectedly. Everyone had to stop for a moment and briefly consider the immense wonder of the universe before they were overwhelmed by the ordinary again. I went out and found Charlie, who was supposed to be putting up a fence, admiring the car. Blackham was actually underneath it, looking at the exhaust manifold. It was the right car for Camilla. She went from one marvellous situation to another at high speed.

Claire was driving a Porsche when I first met her, and wearing short skirts. When we met my main means of getting around had been my aeroplane but I hadn't really ever owned a car. Since Claire's BMW got toasted on the very first day, I'd eventually picked up a seven-seater. She'd gone through her whole life without ever noticing a Volvo. She said, 'What's that?' inquisitively. I said, 'It's a Volvo. It was only, er, two thousand guineas.' Actually it was two thousand one hundred quid, off a bloke in Stoke, but I had to do something to make it sound more appealing to her. She took to wearing trousers as a protest. Camilla had politely declined to get in it and she and Claire followed us to the nursery school sports day in the mean machine.

I remember my dad marvelling at the turning circle of his Volvo estate. Turning circle wasn't a category that figured in 'Top Trumps' but he was really pleased about it, I remember very clearly. Sure enough when we went the wrong way for the third time we pulled a nifty one-eighty while the girls, who were following, struggled with a three-point turn in the narrow country lane. I guess, somewhere in the middle of that swift U-turn as I marvelled at how the car swung around, I became my dad and arrived at middle age, in the back of a whirling Volvo. There it was. The turning performance was truly magnificent. There was no doubt about it. 'Great turning circle innit?!' I shouted down to my father-in-law in the cockpit. I was with a two-year-old in the bit right at the back, where the dogs go. He was driving. 'It's bloody brilliant,' he said. Of course, driving a Volvo was making him feel young again.

Camilla whizzed off to the next party as my friend Matthew arrived with his fiancée in a beautiful vintage Jag. They'd only just got engaged and I couldn't help wondering what they'd be sailing around in, the next time they came.

A lot of people who lived in the country thought they would be lucky to spend a day in London without getting menaced, mugged or murdered. Fred had never been to London, would never go to London, and was proud of it. He was quite happy manhandling a moody bull, armed with just a small piece of wood, but for him, a man whose entire life was a breach of health and safety guidelines, the place suggested nothing but risk and violence. It was a complete misapprehension of course. There's nowhere safer to be in the entire nation than Greater London.

The view of the country from the city is just as misconstrued. When I lived in London, the countryside appeared to be a place where nothing ever happened, where everything came to rest. Outsiders only ever get snapshots. Landscape paintings and photographs of trees and flowers are misleading. Television can't capture the glacial dynamics of nature, either. Even dropping in for a picnic occasionally before I lived here wasn't enough to get an impression of how much things changed. Everything happens fast in towns and cities. Nothing is still. Cars go fast, shops are busy, people rush around: you can see all the parts moving. The countryside always suggests complete stillness by comparison. It is actually a massive green engine. The view out of the window is different every day. When it rains the whole thing changes colour. It took a little while to sink in before it properly dawned on me that absolutely everything, the whole shebang, is always moving.

* * *

I suppose the biggest difference between what I thought living in the country would be like, and what it actually was like, was the amount of time I had on my hands. It usually took between ten and a hundred times longer to get things done than I could have possibly imagined, and usually involved ten times as many people and cost a hundred times as much. That shouldn't have come as a surprise. It would be nice to sit back and just watch it all, I thought sometimes, but it was completely impossible. I couldn't help fiddling with everything. It was even harder to do nothing in Oxfordshire than it was in Soho.

I even started liking Beethoven. Actually, I made it happen, same way as I made myself like oysters: perseverance. I decided to listen to his First Symphony every day for ten days at high volume and see what happened. Around about the seventh or eighth day the thing was permanently playing in my head. As I wandered around the place, the entire English countryside transformed in my mind into a monster budget video commissioned specifically to accompany his music. I was inside a perfect film hearing imaginary violins and oboes, beguiled – sometimes to a standstill – by the excellence and variety of the colour green or the exactness of sunshine on alliums, with their subtle garnish of sheep in the middle distance and a host of imaginary violins. I'd have rather liked to be left alone for long enough to go peacefully insane like everybody else.

But the lovely bubble would always burst. Usually by Fred wandering up and saying something like 'Another one of them tups 'as 'ad it.' And I was back down to earth. As much as I would have liked to float around, there was always something or someone slapping me back to my senses and to my surprise I seemed to be the most sensible person I could find. Sometimes I'd still feel overwhelmed by the scale of the place, cowed by how far it was from the tip of the mast to where I stood. I was always at the helm of this huge ship, one eye on the horizon, and the vast, relentless momentum of the thing lent intense beauty to the occasional moments of apparent perfect stillness in the foreground, especially when Beethoven was involved.

The best thing about Saturday summer lunches was raiding the strawberry patch. I'd checked the strawberries the day before and there were a couple of hints of orange, but the sun had been out since and quickly painted them all bright red, the best red I've ever seen: it was unmistakably 'eat me' red. I'd planted quite a lot of strawberries because I couldn't remember anything I'd ever liked better than picking strawberries. Surrounded by them in an avalanche, the first fruits of an entire winter and spring of messing around with everything from ten-tonne excavators to trowels, felt better than it ever had. The children, especially the two smallest ones, who'd never seen fruit in its natural habitat, were in ecstasies of sunshine and stickiness.

It doesn't always make it easier, having food growing in the garden, though. It all comes at once. The early tomatoes were ripe as well, and after giving the vegetable beds and fruit trees the once over, Claire decided there were some onions that were worth having and some apples. I was having a good shot at doing nothing and enjoying it with even more relish than usual. But she wanted the step ladders. She had to have them. Then she wanted some bags, then she wanted me to hold the ladder and the bag, then she wanted a trowel, and a basket – and then one of the kids wanted a trowel too. I was about to fly off the handle.

I stomped back to the vegetable garden with trowel-type onion retrievers just as a hot air balloon floated past, very low and large. There was hardly any breeze and it was a victory for the serene and the immaculate. There is something about a hot air balloon passing close by that makes everyone want to run after it. The toddler had dropped her strawberries and was shouting 'Bawoon! Big big bawoon!' and involuntarily moving towards it, mesmerised. Claire and I ran over the fields as it gently climbed over the trees and slipped away in slow motion.

The next day, and Sunday lunch had been going on for most of the afternoon. There were only the treacle tarts still to come when the roar of an aircraft engine shook the house to bits. 'Tony!' said everyone and ran outside. Sure enough it was my old flying instructor in a borrowed aeroplane. He was lining himself up for another low pass, landing gear and flaps down. He made a very slow orbit at tree-top height. I could see him clearly in the cockpit, grinning. The landing gear went back up, the engine roared and he whizzed past again at bullet speed, pulling into a climb as he cleared the house. The aeroplane didn't make me want to run after it. It rooted me to the spot. I found myself hankering after one again.

The original red brick garden wall had been breaking my heart for years. It was ancient as it was beautiful as it was long and it was slowly falling over, mainly because of the trees that had overrun the far side of it. Many builders had looked at that wall, shaken their heads and pulled their serious faces. Two architects had told me the best thing to do would probably be to knock it down and start again, but it was perfect as it was. It would have cost an unthinkable amount to rebuild anyway. You couldn't get bricks like that any more. It was so long and so high, and it had been there so long it had become part of the landscape. It had espaliered peach trees growing up it, honeysuckle and an ancient grape vine. Birds nested in it.

I'd given up on it – it was propped up along most of its length with scaffolding poles. Then a very old man with bright white hair and three brown teeth appeared and asked if I wanted the wall sorting out. His name was Ray. He was from a gypsy family and he persuaded me to let him try. He took off the top three rows of bricks and used them to make piers to support the thing. A few weeks later it looked like it would last another five hundred years – as long as no one planted anything too close to it. What a source of joy it was, to be confronted every morning by something that had been falling down for years, all patched up and made lovely again.

Some things got fixed and some things broke. I built an outside shower, cheaper on paper than an indoor one, and I thought, the best way to deal with five muddy kids. A week after it was finished, it exploded and became a magnificent fountain. We watched it for a while, then I switched it all off at the isolator, to the dismay of the children. 'Why's there a fountain? What's a gasket? Where's the fountain gone?' It occurred to me, not for the first time as a tank full of hot water cascaded down the windows of the playroom, that at least when nothing worked or happened here, things were simple. When nothing worked, there was nothing to go wrong. The shower had only been operational for a week and except for me, no one had used it yet. Blackham had been back in the shed tweaking the quad bike for as long as I could remember. The more I fixed, the more things there were to go wrong. If stuff would just have stayed fixed, it would have been fine, but sometimes it all seemed to be slipping through my fingers.

I loved watching the flowers grow with the sunshine on my face but it often occurred to me over the years that just walking into a shop and buying food was actually quite a good arrangement. Buying things retail is easier than trying to create it all from first principles but it was hard to know what I was going to love until I tried. I'd had no great hopes for chickens, but they just cockadoodled around affirming life *in excelsis* from the moment they arrived, while surviving almost entirely on leftovers. The very thought of not having chickens would be terrifying. It would be like not having a car. Everyone should have a couple of chickens.

And then, according to *Forbes* magazine, Burford, Oxfordshire, was the sixth best place to live in Europe. Claire had taken me there the very first time we visited the Cotswolds. It was our third date. I remember laying eyes on the place very clearly. Freefalling through a perfect picture after a right turn off the A40, all mossy slate and honeyed gables running down a hillside to a stream, a sense of butchers, bakers, bric-a-brac and green. I had the feeling that we'd arrived somewhere as the air-cooled engine of her Porsche roared impolitely along the high street, turning heads.

Up to that moment, my first glimpse of Burford, I'd thought I'd only find paradise abroad somewhere. Until recently, happy ever after meant moving far away. Everyone wanted to run away to Provence and never come back. I'd thought I'd probably end up living in France or Argentina, New York or the South Seas, I hadn't really ever decided, but in the two minutes it took to travel through Burford and cross the Windrush on the far side, something had changed. I hadn't said a word. The engine was so loud it was impossible to talk, but she was smiling and so was I. I knew that I had found the woman I wanted to spend the rest of my life with and the place where I wanted to spend it.

Burford is overwhelmingly somewhere that shouts, 'Stop!' But I rarely do, because it is impossible to park there. In the 1950s, it was practically a ghost town. Half of the houses were unoccupied. Now it was booming. The people of Burford were all secretly pleased to get one over on Kingham on the international stage, but the people of Kingham were magnanimous. *Forbes* suggested it would be nicer to live in Tuscany, anyway. That was the number one place, for them. They were wrong. I have been there and there is no grass. No grass, no daisies and they haven't invented any new cheeses for hundreds of years. I mean, great for a holiday, but if there's one thing that's better than being on holiday, it's being at home.

'I'll have another track through here,' I said, 'going down to the river over the old railway bridge and why don't you go round the pond as well. That'll be nice. We'll be able to see it again.' There was a plant hire firm doing special opening deals and Blackie had hired a machine that ate new roads out of undergrowth, an enormous, ride-on beard clipper. No sooner said than done. Some trim: that very evening I was zooming around completely new geography on the quad bike – Blackie had had a good week. Impenetrable, head-high thickets of jumbling bramble, thistle and nettles had been razed to a flat, earthy rug. Butterflies rising on either side of me as I passed in top gear with the whippet in hot pursuit.

I still hadn't been able to put the eight acres with a river along one side to any practical use. It was beautiful, though, still my favourite field: a secluded wilderness, somewhere else altogether where no one ever went except me. The first and last of the day's sunshine smashed into my face as I flew out of the woodland at the bottom of the valley and into the field. A large deer stood on the pristine new track by the river, momentarily as frozen as a picture, then the whole scene exploded. The whippet executed a gear change and flew round me like a Bentley passing a bus on the A40. Shouting at him to stop, I chased the whippet, the whippet chasing the bolting deer all along the river – all of us in flight in the immaculate serenity of high summer in the middle of nowhere. The deer made good its escape over a stile at the far end of the field. 'Don't do that again,' I said to the dog, as he chewed another butterfly, but I could tell he wasn't listening.

Best of all in the summer was the bonfire. It always was just a bit too cold to sit out in the garden in the evenings. I don't know why I hadn't thought of it before, but a fire was all it took to make the difference. A few well-placed rocks around it, and a guitar. It was even quite nice in the rain. I'd talked myself into building just one more kitchen, outside near the bonfire: a very modest one. Blackie called his mate Neil, and he turned up with his girlfriend. She was the first buildeuse I'd ever met. They worked together. We built a ramshackle kitchen in the garden out of bits that were lying around, with a range for burning logs made out of old fence posts and pieces of zinc. It had a tin roof and a water supply pumped straight from the well.

* * *

I was having dinner in grander surroundings on the other side of the valley. The big houses all took it in turns to fire up their kitchens. It was a long table in a huge dining room. It was roaring. I was just having a moment to myself, half considering the man opposite me, when I overheard him tell someone that he was a doctor. I often wondered what to call myself in those kind of situations. I often told people I was a farmer but very few people really know what that means. I suppose it's anyone involved with the land but it's pretty vague. Prince Charles is a farmer. Fred is a farmer too, but they didn't have that much in common. Having said that, they probably would have talked about pigs for some time if they'd ever met.

There were three brothers who'd just inherited the farm at the bottom of the hill. I went to say hello and give them some cheese. They were so enthusiastic about it. They were already getting down to business. I spotted that one of them had really black hands and I stopped talking mid-sentence. I'm not sure how many farmers I'd met by now, a good many: woodsmen, dairymen, combine operators, arable gamblers, pig princes, vegetable growers, a whole lot – but this was the first time I'd seen anyone with soil on his hands. Modern farmers are like conductors – they don't touch anything. They just make it all happen. In the twenty-first century so many of the tasks of agriculture are performed by machines and the whole life-cycle of a grain of wheat, or even a pint of milk, happens without anyone getting dirty hands (in fact dairy farmers have the cleanest hands of anyone you'll ever meet).

It had been good to see the old cowshed back in business. It had been full of huffing, pregnant Gloucesters over the winter. Now there were more in the front field, but these ones had no udders, something that I only realised when I took the children in to say a friendly hello. The entire herd, maybe a couple of dozen of them, had been lying down, and it was only when they started to stand up and stare – looking moodier than the Chippy hoodies – that it dawned on me they must be the other type of cow.

In any flock of sheep there is always one that is slightly braver than all the others but when a lamb starts staring and trying to look tough it's quite funny. It's not unheard of, but a ram had never tried to pick a fight with me. There are mushrooms that are more frightening to behold than a sheep with attitude. It's hard for something so soft and fluffy to come over as tough. In the scheme of all God's creatures, sheep, especially really young ones, are comparatively bold and inquisitive. It was nice being tailed by large groups of them as I walked around the place; most things you encounter in the fields are timid. All one usually sees of deer and rabbits are their back ends. They live on their nerves, wild animals.

Fear was not something these bull calves lived with at all. I could tell that straight away, so I dispatched the children gingerly and went back later with Paddy. 'They definitely had udders before, when they were in the barn,' I said, 'they were pregnant, too.' 'Yes, the pregnant cows have gone,' he said, 'these are the steers. Beef. It's best to have a large-ish stick when you approach these boys.' We had no stick, and stopped walking towards them when they were all on their feet. The bull is the undisputed king of the agricultural jungle: the biggest, strongest, toughest thing in the kingdom – and they know it. They didn't want any trouble, but they were ready for it. They speak fluent body language: 'Come on then, just try coming a bit closer and see what happens,' they were saying. We kept a respectful distance. Humbling creatures.

The professor who ran the Royal Agricultural College in Cirencester asked if he could come over with a group of inner city kids who'd shown an interest in becoming farmers. He said it would be nice to see Cornflake, too. They arrived mid-afternoon a couple of weeks later. Wide-eyed, whispering, clasping their packed lunches they poured out of the college minibus and assembled obediently, timidly in the yard in the sunshine. They looked really cool, hoodies and jeans with new wellies: easily the coolest farmers I'd ever seen. I would have willingly bought fruit and vegetables from them there and then.

They gathered around me and I began to explain the history of the farm, pointing out various features, ancient wells, walls and woodlands. Just as I was getting to the Enclosure Act of 1801, the exciting bit, I spotted Fred ambling around and beckoned him to come over. Here was a bona fide expert, a man of the soil, of the field – an award-winning husband of nature to enlighten them, right on cue. I introduced him to everybody and asked him if he would say a few words about his sheep.

'Well, them ewe lambs just 'bout last 'em. Got them tups up in yard 'spose. Ooh, aren't them buggers, though! Eh? … Goh!' Just then Ray, the snaggle-toothed wall genius, who had found all kinds of ways of making himself useful and had more or less moved in since finishing the garden wall, managed to fire up the circular saw. It had been play-ing up all morning. He'd been having a good old fiddle with it but we'd all more or less given up on the thing. Now it was clearly back in business and Ray was waving it around for joy with a blissful toothless grin on his face, drowning out Fred's authentic rustic oratory.

'Maybe we'll go crayfishing,' I shouted over the din, grabbing the nets and heading for the river. 'Bit of farm business diversification. It's a free crop. It's a nice walk. There are sheep on the way. They're fairly self-explanatory, really, sheep, you'll see.'

Excitement about the American crayfish that were colo-nising the river grew every year in the village. Three people had already called specifically to tell me that it was nearly crayfish season, and any idle gate-post chat soon blew round to the subject. Everyone had a view on the crayfish. Blackham was the undisputed king of crayfishing. Even Paddy deferred to him. Almost everyone agreed that bacon was necessary as bait but some people used nets, some used cage traps. My dad had become intrigued and was doing very good business with a lobster pot that he got from a fisherman in Poole and adapted.

The top field had just been cropped for hay, and was looking spectacularly good. Suddenly it was high summer, one of those bright days that made it obvious why billionaires have always lived on farms, why pop stars buy them to live happily ever after on, why it might be better mucking about making bonfires and gazing at the horizon, like Fred does, rather than staring at a computer screen and wondering whether to have a sandwich or sushi for lunch. It's a hard sell in the modern world, agriculture, but the butterflies and dragonflies were skipping on the hedgerows, everything was out. It was busy. It was beautiful, wherever you came from.

'Is dat your tree?'

'Yep, I guess so.'

'Izzit? How can you like own … a tree? Cooool! How much is it? This place.'

'Well, you can rent the fields for twenty-five quid an acre a year, at least Fred does. I throw the trees in.'

I'd been looking forward to seeing the river. I never got down there often. It was flowing steadily and purposefully towards London. We baited up the nets, threw them in the river and tucked into sandwiches in the long grass by the waterside, brushing away the buzzers and bombers. The kids were enthusiastic, inquisitive and completely and involuntarily engaged with it all, suddenly. They asked the professor endless questions that led to more questions and he sprinkled his expertise over them delicately like seasoning for the sandwiches.

We caught four crayfish. Not a huge success, but I think agriculture won a few hearts. Sometimes it's hard to see why anyone would want to do anything else.

CHAPTER 11

HIGH DAYS AND HOLIDAYS

The village fete was busy. It had everything. Pretty girls, maypole dancing, egg and spoon, fancy dress, the full nine yards. I judged the fancy dress. So much work had gone into the costumes. That sort of style doesn't come off the shelf. It was couture, beyond anything off the peg in Bond Street shop windows. It was an immaculate parade. Love and care had trumped anything money could have bought. There was a girl dressed and painted orange, with whiskers and a tail made out of tights: impressive. 'I'm Puss in Boots,' she stated – and pouted.

I asked a Professor Dumbledore if he had come far but he started to cry. There was a Spiderman whose mother had already approached me, to point out details of his outfit – trying to influence the decision making process. There was a Wimbledon champion, a shivering synchronised swimmer and a moustachioed, stripey strong man with papier-mâché dumbbells. There were numerous fairies, princesses and angels, but first prize went to an elaborate pantomine horse and rider collaboration. The horse's back legs were so excited the whole thing collapsed in a heap.

The locals were playing 'Aunt Sally': an immensely tricky, deadly serious throwing game involving different shaped sticks. There was skittles. There were coconuts. There was 'Splat the Rat': a blousy lady stood behind a flapping silk flag and whizzed the rats (made from old tights) down a length of pipe. There was a Quality Street for anyone who could whack the rat mid-air with a rounders bat as it came flying out at the bottom. She was a mean pitcher. I got two coconuts but I couldn't get anywhere near the rats.

The kids disappeared. Some went up the greasy pole and others were smashing plates so I went to the big marquee for some extra-strong tea and a fat slice of quiche. I sat next to a beaming pair of seniors, and showed them my coconuts. The sun came out and the Silver Band were playing tunes I hadn't heard since I was a child: 'The Floral Dance', 'Captain Beaky'. Powerful to hear forgotten music in the sunshine, and as the three-legged races started I drifted off, calm, content and at home.

I've felt it about the whole of Manhattan, parts of Paris, and one or two restaurants in London. Bournemouth beach in high summer has it. So do helicopters, Daylesford, and a six-foot circle around Stephen Fry: glamour. The things and the places that make the whole of the rest of the world seem a bit flat by comparison. Not always, but now and then, the farm had glamour. Sometimes all it took was for the sun to come out. There might be no one else here at all, just me, the dogs and a handful of sheep in the middle distance and suddenly it seemed that the whole of the rest of the world was irrelevant, unappealing. Rain, blazing bonfires and good company could all cast the magic spell, too.

By now, I'd imagined I would have learnt the Latin name for tomatoes, tried my hand at dowsing, spent cheery, hopeful afternoons looking for treasure with a metal detector and endless evenings peering through telescopes, but as the months went by I found I had less and less time for anything remotely wafty. I became more and more driven: honed to a fine edge; a flurry of cut, thrust and hustle. On the phone with a mouthful, bolting down lunch, cutting a deal with a dodgy scaffolder, my eyes engaged elsewhere, darting back and forth over the Ordnance Survey plans of the land – boldly coloured to show where we'd be planting several thousand trees before the end of the next month. It occurred to me as I negotiated with the scaffolder with one part of my brain, how easy it would be to plant an entire forest in the wrong place. I had a feeling the owner before last had decided to chop an entire forest down while thinking about something else.

Claire woke me up to say that the steers had escaped again and this time they were eating the neighbour's garden. 'You know what to do,' I said, half-asleep. Why didn't Fred shut that gate? 'Yes, I've done it. They're back. It's all fine, just thought you'd like to know. I'm going to London now. Bye,' she said, and off she went, in a whirl of her own. Running the farm was totally absorbing. It had its own gravity. I worked from home and I never wanted to leave. As the machine became more sophisticated and more and more things began to happen simultaneously, it was ever harder to tear myself away. It did take all day, every day to run the place and I needed a break but the more I thought about going on holiday, the less I wanted to leave. I didn't want to miss the plums again. That was a disaster. It didn't feel like summer had been fully realised without the sweet, fat exclamation marks of more plums than I could possibly know what to do with. The irrepressible bounty of them, the way they cascaded into readiness, crash and burn, filled me up with joy. There'd only been a few soggy ones left the time we'd got back from Bournemouth and I'd felt empty. If it hadn't been the plums it would have been something else I'd miss.

I had to take a week off, though. I'd had a look at a few options but it was high season and high prices; it was horrible. I thought, 'My God, we could just stay here and live like princes for that.' I asked the kids where they wanted to go. Two of them said the sandpit and that sealed it. Suddenly it all made perfect sense. They didn't want to go anywhere either. Home is where the trampoline, the swing and all their toys are. If we stayed, I wouldn't miss the peaches or any of the figs. I could teach the puppy some tricks. I could do exactly what I wanted, and so could the kids. Obviously we'd need to go further than the bottom of the garden one day but for now the twins were still fascinated by more or less everything. They didn't care where they were. 'Darling,' I said, 'let's stay right here.' 'I'm going to get a driver and a chef. Get yourself a masseuse and whatever else you want. We'll be up to our necks in luxury and we'll still be quids in and we'll be here.' We were in England in July for goodness sake. Why would we want to go anywhere?

There was some asbestos to deal with, but it could wait another week, as long as the dog stopped chewing it. Hell, it could all wait. I finished work early on Friday, shut up my shed and checked into my room. The cleaner had put a bunch of flowers on the bedside table. It was instantly clear that it was the nicest hotel I've ever stayed in. It was so easy to get to as well. I thought of the crowds at Heathrow and felt very clever. Claire was still at work in London. The kids were all napping. I lay on the bed and wondered where to start. Anticipation is the sweetest pleasure. There was a whole catalogue of things I wanted to do, all the things I never had time for: actually figuring out exactly how my telescope worked, going to the wildlife park and staying until they fed the lions at dusk, finding the cricket pitch, digging up the medieval village. I wrote a list. I wouldn't have time to do everything I wanted, but it was a nice list to write.

Doing nothing is quite different from having nothing to do. Having nothing to do is plain boredom. Idleness is a choice, an exquisite realm. What I needed more than anything was a rest I realised, as sunshine streamed onto my closed eyelids.

I think the two greatest luxuries a man can have are new socks every day, and a nap in the afternoon. I made a mental note to buy some socks and dozed off.

The summer sunshine was beautiful but I was nowhere near as fussy about the weather as I used to be. I'd come to enjoy all aspects of it, rain was my current favourite condition, but Claire arrived home to a conventional high summer scorcher. The haze mellowed into orange as swallows leant on the stillness, dragonflies poked the echinacea and the dog trotted round with his bone. I'd only been on holiday for three hours and already I was showing signs of going feral myself, running round in bare feet, making a bonfire to cook on.

I'd always thought it would be amazing to have a chef, but realised I wanted nothing more than to do the cooking myself. It wasn't a chore. It was a joy. The washing up was a different matter though, so the au pair did some overtime.

I was having a great time and it was Monday, and I still hadn't spent any money. Didn't even know where my wallet was. We were even saving on fuel as I was cooking on the bonfire. It was time to burn some holiday cash. Another great thing about being at home on holiday was that I knew where all the shops were, so I could be a lot more discerning about buying holiday grot. All the stuff I had to pay for on holiday usually – stuff we'd forgotten to pack, airport taxes, Toblerones – we could have a proper splurge instead, get some properly useful junk. I called the local chauffeur company and said I wanted to go to Oxford via Toys-R-Us as soon as possible. There was a stretch at the door in fifteen minutes.

I wanted to go to Oxford. I wanted to feel Oxford, be a part of that whirring occult machinery. Oxford was always something I felt I should be having a bit more of. Along with going for long walks, writing to my granny, taking photographs, braising, learning the names of birds and their tunes: going to Oxford languished on my 'would like to do' list. I was still a complete stranger in that city, even though I'd worked there. Everything happened so fast there. I'd never managed to find the stillness that I enjoyed in London, the sense of repose that comes with belonging somewhere. I'd tried to linger but lunch never took more than twenty minutes. Everyone had always gone before I'd had time to think of anything to say. Even dinner had only lasted half an hour in December. It was like being in a mad narrow-gauge train set where everything happened quicker than normal. I'd even tried staying at the Randolph Hotel, but when I woke up, all I could think about was the car.

Parking in Oxford is a number. It's a city centre that predates the wheel. In London, parking is never really a problem. It's expensive and never glamorous but you can, always. Sometimes in Oxford you just can't. Can't park, anywhere. The last time I'd gone there was on a Sunday evening and the only space I could find meant Claire had to get out before I wedged it in, and I had to exit through the driver's window. We got to the theatre late. Oxford wasn't designed around the car. It was all squashed into a tiny space, like lunch. Being driven around is one of the perks of working in the music business. It's right up there in the new socks, class-A category of delicious pleasures. It was even better for not particularly having to go anywhere. I figured we'd spend the cost of our kids' flights on toys, but it was soon obvious we'd need a lorry if we wanted to do that. They were going mental by the time we'd filled our first trolley. Slip'n'slide, paddling pools, flying machines, bubble machine – and that was just my stuff. Even with the boys' haul, it still came to less than the cheapest no frills flight out of Luton. In fact, going bananas in a toyshop while the chauffeur waited was cheaper than getting to Luton and parking the car there for a week.

With the boot full of toys we rode into the city centre. I do love Oxford. It's a kind of heaven, heaven with no parking. Girls on bicycles, glimpses of secret quadrangles, someone playing the bagpipes, or maybe a harpist on the High Street, depending what day it was; the bookshops and Blackwell's Music.

We got out and marched on down the High Street to Magdalen Bridge where the punts are kept. 'Who wants to go on a boat with Daddy?' One of the twins showed some inclination, but only because he thought it was the only way to get back to the toyshop. I'd carried this dream of a sunny day's punting with the family through the whole winter. It was what had kept body and soul together. The day was here and there was no one at the boathouse. Then it started to rain.

We walked along the Isis getting wet. There was too much goose poo for the children to avoid waddling through a fair amount of it. Children can't reasonably be expected to look where they are going. A scary-looking man in a stained tracksuit was playing Frisbee with his extra-large dog with one hand and drinking Tennents Super with the other. On the river a couple of beautiful women sculled silently past. I suppose that is Oxford in a nutshell, the loud and repulsive on one side, the quiet and sublime on the other – in the rain. We were sitting under the canopy of St John's boathouse when a couple wobbled past on a punt. They were not having a good time. She was wearing a pretty dress, which was soaking. He was doing his best, but going nowhere and probably as worried about what was going to happen to his car as what she was thinking. I'm pretty sure anything that's parked for more than an hour gets towed away and crushed. Oxford had crushed them completely. Still, it meant the punt hire shop had opened and I persuaded most of the kids and one of the nannies aboard and soon we were punting up a side stream. It was all pretty murky. The smaller children wanted to pull slimy things out of the water. 'Put it BACK! It's dirty,' I barked. There were tears.

Punting is tricky. It's like trying to park a bus that has had its engine and steering wheel replaced with a long matchstick. I always nearly fall in. I'd never actually fallen in. Maybe that was why I felt so confident. The pole got stuck in the mud, I gave it a good yank and flew spectacularly off the back and took a complete header in the dirtiest stretch of the dirtiest river in Europe. Underneath the slimy surface it actually felt quite clean and refreshing as I paddled back towards daylight. The kids were howling with delight. The nanny was crying, she was laughing so much. The au pair was trying to take a photo. A couple walking their dog had never seen anything quite so amusing. The sun was shining. Suddenly everything was all right. We went and had milkshakes.

I particularly like the butchers in the covered market. There is an excellent greengrocer, too; outfitters shops: green cords, wellies and tweed. It was all absolutely world class and all absolutely empty, because it was July and everyone had gone on holiday. The fools. I loaded up on holiday reading at Blackwell's. *The Complete Sherlock Holmes*, *The Geology of Oxfordshire*, *The Music of the Primes*, a yard of poetry, and a breezeblock of P. G. Wodehouse.

Back at home I got stuck into Sherlock in the afternoon sun, while the dog and the children played in their new world of brightly-coloured fantastic plastic. The toys were great while they lasted, but by the next morning the paddling pool had a puncture, we'd run out of bubble juice and the Slip'n'slide was leaking; so we were back to squirting each other with the hose like we usually did. That is the best fun anyway.

Claire booked a reflexologist who squeezed her toes and told her not to eat bread. Ridiculous. I opted out of reflexology and had a sandwich instead. The au pair painted my toenails gold. Then the psychic came. He flipped his cards around and said next June would be good. Various grandparents arrived. My dad and I caught some crayfish. My mum picked the peaches. Claire went horse riding. Claire's mum assembled a Lego digger that I was rather looking forward to building. Claire's dad listened to Elvis. I called all the people that I haven't spoken to for ages. I took lots of naps and bought some socks. I didn't get close to boredom or thinking about work. I had hoped that I might get round to tidying up my shed, but it didn't even cross my mind. I was in a different mode, altogether. We drifted happily through the days. We went to a steam rally and watched the working ferrets, the steam-rollers and the tractor parade, and left nauseous from too much candy floss and helter skeltering. We didn't get to the wildlife park. We didn't go out much at all, really. The weather held out and so did the hosepipe. By way of a climax, I invited an astronomer and his girlfriend for dinner on the last night to help figure out how the intelligent telescope worked. It was a crisp and clear evening and we had a good look at the moon. The moon is somewhere that I would be prepared to go on holiday.

The auto-align functions of the telescope even baffled my learned friend. The telescope seemed to think that Jupiter was in the hay barn. We were just getting the hang of it as a low bank of stratus arrived and obscured the whole of the heavens. It was good while it lasted, though. The sheer miraculousness of everything is never so blatantly apparent as it is to two men who have got together with a new telescope. We'd got ourselves quite excited and needed to come in and calm down anyway.

I went to bed with a firm grasp of my place in the universe and got back to business the next morning reinvigorated, rejuvenated and ready for asbestos removal. I couldn't imagine how we could have had a better time.

Since pre-civilisation high summer has been the time when all the big feasts and celebrations have taken place. There were local festivals that stretched back into the mists of time: all kinds of unmissable events and extravaganzas.

The Royal Show is to agriculture what Glastonbury is to music – with the Brit awards thrown in, a chaotic and benign extravaganza. The whole industry converging for everyone to measure up against each other and have a few drinks, with the rest of the world turning up to point and stare. There are many farm shows and they're all a good day out, but 'The Royal' was the big one. The way that teenagers dreamed of being famous one day, farmers dreamed of turning up at the Royal with a promising ewe, sweeping the board with the judges and walking away wearing the 'Champion of Champions' sash, the Holy of Holies. In days gone by a fat contract with a retailer might have followed from a win at The Royal, but it was always winning that mattered most.

To be rich is one thing and probably not that hard if money is all you care about, but to be the very best is never

ever easy. No one who works with animals wants to produce lots and lots of ordinary creatures. They might have to, but it's never anyone's motivation. The reason farmers want to get up in the morning is that they're all trying to make one really good one.

I spent most of the day watching the pig classes, partly because it's the funniest thing I've ever seen. The whole thing teetered delightfully on the brink of collapse. Pigs are always up to something.

When I arrived, a couple of July Large Blacks were trying to have a fight and another one was doing a good job of digging up the turf. There was a couple getting frisky and all the other ones that weren't determined to lie down and go to sleep were trying to escape. The judge stood in the middle of the porky pandemonium wearing a bowler hat and a poker face, all very surreal: a potent mix of pigs, aristocratic landowners, wheeler-dealers and old-fashioned yokels. The handlers wore white coats and held a crook in one hand and a board in the other for wrangling the animals. They were all supposed to parade around the ring in the same direction, but with pigs there is always one that wants to go in the opposite direction to all the others. It is hard to watch pigs without smiling.

The ring had something of the allure of a cricket match. It all unfolded over the course of a nice summer's day and everyone was jolly, but under the surface, incredibly competitive. Fierce whispers, rumours of skulduggery flew around. Word was that one of the Tamworths had been nobbled. There were suggestions that the dead cert for first prize had had a tendon nicked with a razorblade so that she walked with a limp. A judge can't award first prize to a lame animal.

There was only a tiny handful of us watching the pig proceedings but the mirth and high jinks at the beating heart of British agriculture was still apparent in those show rings. The food was frightful – food is always dreadful at agricultural shows. Farming has very little to do with making food really. These events were so precarious. The joy of pigs is subtle and even slightly inclement weather could wreak catastrophe on attendance. I'd promised to take the boys to see the tractor parade at the Oxfordshire Country Fayre. It was pouring with rain but that wasn't enough to dampen the enthusiasm of a three-year-old whose favourite magazine was *Classic Tractor*. It rained all the way there and by the time we arrived the car park was an empty field of sludge. It was raining and blowing so hard between the thunder and the lightning that there was not a soul there except for the participants. There were hundreds of stands, stalls that seemed to be selling everything from lawnmowers to tractors. I found Crudgie but he was already packing up. The terrier racing was a washout – the mud was above head height for terriers and they had all gone home as well. The tractor parade wasn't for another two hours. Claire wanted to see the horses so we went to watch the dressage.

It's often hard to tell how enjoyable things are going to be. It should have been a disaster. I thought I was there for the tractors. The tractors were cancelled but clustered in a

wet huddle watching those dancing horses was more exhilarating than watching New Order re-formed and headlin-
ing Reading Festival in 1998. The riders, young and old, all
immaculately turned out, hurtled over hair-raising jumps,
stuck to their steaming mounts. The foul weather didn't
touch them as they hared around, screamed on by the rest
of their team.

The heaviest rain came in the summer months but on the
whole it was the calmest time of the year. The best thing
about the clement high season was the tent. It was always
called 'the tent', but that didn't do it justice. It was almost
big enough for elephants and tightropes. A big top as big
as a ballroom, lined and interlined like a lush pair of
curtains, utterly ridiculous, but pretty and practical as well.
I loved that tent.

It had belonged to a film director who lived in Burford.
Burford is the sixth nicest place to live in the world but not
a very practical address for a filmmaker, and the time had
come. He said to me, 'You're all right. You make cheese.
You can do that here, but if you're in the oil business,
you've got to live in the Middle East and if you want to
make films, you've got to live in LA.'

Shortly after he left for LA to boss impossible actresses
around, he emailed me, saying I could have the tent. He'd
been directing a huge action sequence with a car chase and
explosions all week, but it had been the tent that he was
thinking about. It was preying on his mind constantly, he
said. He was worried it wouldn't survive the winter in his
shed. 'The pegs are in a big wooden box on the right,' he

explained, 'the sides are in the larger Cambodian canoe and so are the poles. The roof is on the floor in plastic in front of the tractor.' There was an impressive and exhaustive list of instructions, I think probably put together by his producer: for finding the tent, retrieving the tent, how to get the number for the guys who come and put it up and take it down, two combination codes for gates, the code for the lock on the shed.

Having followed all the instructions carefully, I'd found myself standing in his shed, one Sunday morning. It had taken a bit of fiddling around to find the lights: a friendly web of gimcrack wires snaking off in all directions. Even with the lights on, it was quite dim and mysterious in there: a damp cave of brilliant curiosities. No, that couldn't be a Cambodian canoe. It was almost certainly a punt. I lifted some tarpaulin. Still no canoe, instead a gleaming Land Rover, a miniature one. Wow, some shed. There was a strong whiff of WWII about it, asbestos roof and sides, rickety doors and cute wooden windows; all neatly packed and jammed to the gunwales with treasure. I've never been in a shed that isn't full. This one was no exception, full of every big boy's toy imaginable: two perfectly parked ride-on lawnmowers, a gleaming mini tractor and topper attachment, what looked like a couple of Harleys under dust covers at the far end. I didn't want to be too nosey. It seemed quite strange being in someone's shed without them being there. Such an intensely personal place, a shed. You can tell far more about a person from their shed than from their house. The shed is where all the apparatus of joy and half-cooked dreams are kept, inviting comment. Friendly places.

The tent was already going a bit mildewy and smelly. I could tell fetching it was a matter of urgency. The only way I could grab it quickly was by buying a spiral staircase – unseen – from a man who said he could deliver it on his trailer. I said I'd take the stairs if he'd help me with the tent. I just hadn't had time to organise anything more logical. Blackham had a three-wheeler. I called a couple of van people but they wanted to know how big the tent was and all I could tell them was 'really big' and they wanted me to call back with dimensions and volumes which made it all too complicated. I'd pitched it in the garden. The kids saw it and went absolutely bananas. It was full of a bouncy castle and teddy bears in no time and we had been more or less living in it on rugs and cushions ever since, in the garden, but out of the rain. I knew it was where the film director wanted to be, too. It was much more glamorous than Hollywood.

I once met the Crown Prince of Dubai. Of anyone I've ever encountered, I think he had the most. He had every-thing: a yacht as big as Daylesford, a Grand Prix circuit and all of Abba's phone numbers; but I'd take that tent over any of his toys, with the possible exception of the kebab machine at the bottom of his garden. I'd thought it ludicrous, but it turned out a whacking great marquee was actually the most practical, cost-effective slice of heaven going. That was why my friend was so worried about it going mouldy. It wasn't the value of the thing, more that it was something that needed to live on and be enjoyed. The main reason that the tent was so fantastic is because for something so utterly spectacular, it was all so simple. Normally when I wanted to build something I had to start filling in forms. I'd usually have to call a meeting just to find out which forms to fill in. Then there'd be building regulations, wonks, budgets, Blackham, accounts, snags and VAT. Before you know it, it's work. Not with tents. Tents are all play.

I slung an extension cable in there and hooked it up to a kebab machine I bought on eBay.

A spiral staircase had been right at the top of my shopping list for some time, but those particular stairs weren't quite tall enough to reach the first floor of the house. These things are never perfect. Buying second hand always calls for a little bit of creativity and ingenuity. Secondhand stuff has lost all the sheen of its marketing and just exists for what it is. I'd buy everything second hand if I could. Junk shops are just sheds where everything is for sale.

Summer bore on like a tidal wave. Flora sprouting here, there and everywhere: from walls, through concrete, in gutters. The poppies were my favourite. They came up in different spots every year: brilliant random splashes of colour. I tried making them grow but they only ever grew at random. They had their own ideas. It was so pleasant to wander through the calm haze of a poppy filled afternoon. I wandered this way and that, and found myself upstairs in the big derelict stone barn. I wondered for the first time why there were two doors in the wall on the first floor. They were both nailed shut but there was only one door on the other side of that wall. I was sure of it. It was suddenly obvious that there must be quite a large room I'd never known about. I prised open a door that had been fixed shut with ancient nails and stumbled into a dark room that no one had been in for a hundred years.

The Cheese Awards had always been held at the Mill House, the hotel next to the brook that ran through the village. The previous year it had rained so heavily on the day, that over the course of the morning the little brook had grown to a raging torrent. By lunchtime it had burst its banks and flooded the field, and by the time the supreme champion was being judged the tent was waist deep in water and cheeses were floating off towards the village like ducks. I'd offered to hold the awards on the farm. Preparations had been underway for months and as the day drew nearer it got very, very busy: people putting up tents, assembling fridges and air conditioning units. There were lights, trestles, tablecloths. A dilapidated corner of the yard where I'd been keeping piles of things that might come in useful one day, had been completely transformed, terraformed into a billiard table. It had taken three different kinds of excavator. I could hardly contain myself: three excavators and now, an avalanche of every cheese imaginable. It was dream-like.

While I had the excavators I couldn't resist using the little one to trench out a watering system for the vegetable garden. It only had to drive over one hedge to get into the back garden to tap into the well. While laying the pipes for the sprinklers Charlie unearthed another Victorian sewer system underneath the trampoline. Hidden, out of the weather and unused for decades, it was pristine, an immaculately preserved museum piece. It was hard to know what to do with it. It appeared to still be functioning. There was clear spring water running through it. In the end we just covered it up again and hoped we hadn't ruined anything. I'd thought my old digger, the one that had come with the farm, would be able to cope with the rest of the landscaping, but I had to build some new bogs for the judges. I realised I'd need to be ordering something from the deep end of the digger list when the septic tank arrived. I'd dealt with septic tanks before and there is usually nothing nice to say about them. They're not the kind of thing you think about, unless they go wrong. And then it's hard to think about anything else. I'd dug a fairly big hole with my digger, in preparation. It did cross my mind at the time that the hole was about the size of a swimming pool, but the septic tank was probably going to cost marginally more.

When the tank arrived, it was clear I'd underestimated the size. It looked like a nuclear submarine. It was big enough to go to Mars in, as big as a house. The excavator dug a meteorite crater that soon filled up with water from more underground springs. A dozen lorryloads of concrete and a bit of backfilling later, you'd never have known there was anything there. I wondered if anyone would discover it in the distant future and marvel at its beauty.

And so it was that nine hundred and six different kinds of cheese had been counted into the farm one-by-one. It doesn't sound that bewildering, but a good delicatessen probably only carries a couple of dozen varieties. Mayhem, it was. A cavalcade of cars and couriers, crates of the stuff pouring up the drive. From every corner of the kingdom they came, from Cornish Yarg to Orkney Cheddar, Lincolnshire Poacher to a highly-prized hard cheese called Desmond from West Cork. Everything seemed to be working wonderfully, though. The big shed had been transformed into a walk-in humidor, a strange museum of contemporary cheese.

There was a judges' dinner. The most august body of cheese experts it would be possible to imagine, had assembled at The Plough. They traditionally gathered the night before to whet their appetites and share stories. I did have one conversation that almost got on to another subject, something about cigarettes, but everybody wanted to talk about cheese, really. Someone asked me what my favourite cheese was. I paused to answer and realised it was very quiet and everyone was looking at me. I thought about it really hard. It changed all the time. Sometimes I liked Cheddar, sometimes I wanted something really smelly, sometimes only a processed triangle would really hit the spot.

I thought about it and told the truth. 'Well, I seem to be eating rather a lot of ... well, a lot of Gruyère at the moment.' There was a short pause that lasted forever. The cheese buyer from Asda nodded. So did the man who supplied six thousand independent delicatessens with unpasteurised Camembert, and the dreadful silence collapsed into a beautiful rumble of approval. There was much nodding and glances. Generally speaking Gruyère is the most highly-prized cheese among experts. The pasture on the Swiss mountain slopes contains an incredible variety of flora. The cow, the Brown Swiss, produces a relatively small amount of milk, but it is perfect for the cheese – a cheese that has been made in the area, uninterrrupted, for centuries. It was obvious why it was so nice when I thought about it.

By nine-forty-five the next morning, the full judging panel, fifty cheese nutters from home and abroad, had arrived to put the nation's cheeses in the correct order. We had all the eminent cheesemakers – Tom Calver from Westcombe Cheddar, surely in with a good shot at Supreme Champion this year; Joe Schneider, the brains behind Stichelton, the most talked about new cheese for years, also in with a good shout – lined up alongside food writers, wholesalers and various other luminaries to give a full appraisal of the entire cheese situation nationwide as it stood that Friday. Everyone limbered up their taste buds with a few bites of apple. I was happy. And I couldn't really imagine being any happier.

CHAPTER 12

ENCORE

I was heading north with Paddy when I got the call. We were going to Daphne's to shoot grouse. It was dusk. We'd been driving and talking all afternoon and had just reached County Durham. Waves of green landscapes rolling into infinity: it was somewhere else, the edge of another world altogether and we were content and quiet. All my usual concerns, the practicalities and deadlines were on hold for a couple of days. I'd been looking forward to this. As we ground along a single-track road with passing places the phone rang and I tutted and scrabbled around for it in the coat on the seat behind me. It was Blur's manager. He didn't call me often. I said, 'I'd better get this.' And that was the moment everything changed. I couldn't get a word in. He was talking quickly. Excited.

'Look Alex, Graham and Damon have met up. They're mates again and they want to do some gigs. You—'

And then the phone cut out. I'd lost the signal. I tried to call him back but I couldn't get through. It was all very quiet and still on the dusky moor. A grouse moor was about as far removed as anything could be from the noise, the clamour of teeming screaming people, the brilliant, brash chaos of a rock and roll band.

I'd been looking forward to going to County Durham but suddenly it all seemed rather trivial. That phone call kicked everything into touch.

In the last twenty-one years, not a single day had gone by where I hadn't thought about Blur. Every day something would happen that would make the band or one of them cross my mind, or I'd be introduced as 'from Blur' or recognised from those days. And I thought it was never going to happen again. The longer time went on, the less likely it seemed.

These people weren't just my colleagues. They were once my closest friends. I think probably the closest friends I'll ever have and it had been a strange kind of limbo.

Later that week I went to see Damon's latest opera, walked into the after show party, and on the other side of the room with everyone staring at them and whispering about them were Damon and Graham arm-in-arm, like they'd never stopped being best friends. It was all back on. 'Are we going to do some shows then,' said Damon, 'or what?'

There was an offer from a promoter to play in Hyde Park but we all thought it was a gamble putting such a big show on sale after such a long time. It had been ten years and even when Blur had been in full swing we'd never played a gig of that size. There were festivals, but back then bands didn't really do mega-gigs, giga-gigs on their own. When 'Country House' went to number one we did a nationwide tour of five-hundred-capacity end of pier theatres. A lot had changed since then and I think the most wonderful moment of all came just a couple of weeks after that first phone call. I was in the kitchen making breakfast for the children and there was another phone call to say that the Hyde Park show had sold out – sold out in thirty seconds. We'd sold fifty thousand tickets and they were going to add another night. I dropped the wooden spoon in the porridge and cried. I thought the band had been consigned to history, that I was a footballer who'd played his last game. The band was bigger than it had ever been and I'd had no idea, absolutely no idea. We added Glastonbury and some warm-up shows, about a fortnight's worth altogether.

Nothing about my daily life changed, but suddenly everything was different. I was going back to see the herd of Gloucester cows in Bisley. I'd said I'd do an interview with the *Bisley Newsletter* while I was there and they'd wanted to do a photograph. I said that was fine, of course. Suddenly *The New York Times* wanted to come too. I said I'm just going to look at some cows and talk to the lady from the parish council. They seemed to think that was in–credible and a–mazing. Everything had taken on a new significance.

It'd been a while since I'd felt the whirlwind of the media. After *The New York Times*, we were hit by a raging style storm from Italy. At the crack of dawn a lorry and a fleet of Mercedes arrived and disgorged a gallant troupe of high fashionistas. I counted at least thirteen of them, all very glamorous, all wearing jeans and trainers – apart from the photographer who was wearing an impossible kind of wellington slipper that I instantly hankered after. It's alluring, fashion, that's the point of it. It was go, go, go go from the moment they arrived. The styling team had brought so many clothes the wardrobe department had to set up in the tomato shed. There just wasn't enough space in the house. Hair and make-up used the big lounge. I wasn't allowed in there. 'Do not TOUCH! His hair is *perfetto*,' said the photographer. The hair stylist made a move to adjust my fringe. 'NO! NO!' cried the photographer, and then, 'YES, YES, YES! Is beautiful! STOP! We shoot right now. I LOVE it.'

I liked that guy.

The clothes used in fashion shoots are all catwalk size. No other sizes exist. My feet have always been too big for fashion shoes, they give me cramps and blisters, but to my surprise, I could still get into most of the other stuff. There was, though, a very tight couture waistcoat that I was struggling to fasten. The stylist took a pair of scissors and cut straight up the back, completely trashing it with one hand whilst fastening the buttons at the front with the other. He was a flurry of finesse, had me dressed in about two minutes. He ripped open the tacked-together breast pocket of the blazer he had been sporting over his arm, whilst adjusting the waistcoat, deftly whipping a handkerchief arrangement in there, simultaneously tying a knot I'd never seen before in an exceptionally skinny tie. I thought he was going to cry when I didn't want to wear any of the dozens of trainers, but we compromised. The photographer had set up in the muddy bit, down by the sheep barn. A sound system had been installed from nowhere and the rest of the gang were down there tapping their feet and sipping smoothies. It looked like a really cool party. Fred was there but he wasn't dancing.

The photographer's two assistants seemed to be working the hardest of all. The photographer shot hundreds of frames on many different cameras, so they were reloading, labelling, constantly taking light readings, changing settings, moving tripods. They were all outstandingly good at their jobs. The photographer knew exactly what he wanted and had them very well organised. He was out of this world. He said sheep were 'sooo boooring', said that he used to have a pet puma but now he kept hawks in the castle where he lived in Marrakech.

Claire arrived fresh from the glamour squad, looking amazing head-to-toe in John Richmond, apart from the wellies. 'Now I want you to kiss. Oh my God don't stop. Is amaaazing. Quick give me my Leica. I want to shoot this right now.' We shot half a dozen completely different looks in less than three hours. That's really going some. It's Olympic speed. Then whoosh, they were gone as quick as they'd arrived. It was properly glamorous. It felt like there was something indefinable that was missing when they'd left, like the day after Christmas or the feeling I always get when I'm leaving New York, the emptiness after waking from a really good dream. If I didn't have the pictures to prove it, I'd have thought it was.

When I arrived at the first rehearsal Graham was there already, playing the guitar surprisingly quietly, but he looked the same and sounded the same as he did the last time we'd rehearsed, ten years ago. Dave the drummer walked in and started banging the drums and fiddling with them like drummers always do. Twiddling the nuts on cymbals and tightening things. Damon arrived and he just nodded, grinned and said, 'Shall we try "Beetlebum", then?' From Graham's opening riff, straight away it sounded just like the record and I was tingling as I found myself catapulted to the day the song was written in 1995, when I'd just got back from New York City not having slept for three days. I'd forgotten all about it, but that was just the first of a million memories. All of a sudden the miraculous house of cards was somehow standing again. We went over absolutely everything. It had been such a long time. I'd had no children then. I'd not even met Claire, the last time the four of us had played together. None of my children had any idea I was ever in a band.

There was a lot of ground to cover, seven albums plus various singles and dozens of B-sides and we played absolutely everything. We rehearsed once a week and to start with we played one album in its entirety each week, plus slung in a few B-sides. It was strange. Sometimes I was nineteen years old again. Sometimes I felt a hundred and four. Songs that I hadn't thought about at all, that I'd completely forgotten about, triggering unexpected avalanches of memory: the album *Modern Life Is Rubbish*, the most. Those songs from before the party started, when we were young, when we had nothing to lose, when we were all as poor as church mice. It was all good though. Dazzling to watch Damon deal with backing singers, to bask in Graham's musicality, to realise how much swing there is in the rhythm section, when the brass players – some of them played for the Berlin Philharmonic, the best orchestra in the world – struggled to stay on the grooves.

I used to find rehearsing a drag. Rehearsals and photo shoots were always the most boring aspects of being in a band. Those rehearsals were more enjoyable than anything I'd done for a long time but now there were more photos than ever: photo shoots, film crews, paparazzi, webcams, constant exposure.

Suddenly I had two lives. Back at the farm there were a lot more people coming for lunch than normal. I was having to more or less roast lambs whole. It was still a building site and there were plenty of raw materials lying around for making new barbecues with. I cooked everything under the shade of a birch tree, which only caught fire once. The cooking arrangements were constantly evolving but I was getting very good results with an old iron manger of Fred's which worked well as a base for the coals along with a horrible old well grate that had been hanging around annoying me for ages, but worked brilliantly as a grill. It was a unique thing and uniqueness is gradually being eradicated from the world. I felt free when I stepped back from it. Free from the tyranny of other people's designs. Being a bit rubbish is nothing at all to be scared of. People seemed to love that barbecue even though it was definitely a bit rubbish. Even the people from the big house up the road were impressed. I got another rusty old iron manger from Fred and gave it to them and they took it away with them, chuffed to bits.

I was happy. I had missed lots of things about being in a band but it was important for all four of us to learn how to stand on our own in the world. When the band disintegrated the hardest thing was suddenly being disconnected from my closest friends and what I wanted more than anything was to be in a room with the band, playing those songs again. I didn't care if anyone was watching or not.

I was cured by the end of the rehearsals: I had my friends back. It had never really occurred to me that other people might feel as emotional about the whole thing as I did. Right from the first song of the first gig it was overwhelming. The first show was the tiny Railway Museum where we'd played our first ever gig. A few of the same people were there, too, a lifetime later but this time there were lots of cameras as well. I didn't look down until half way through the first chorus and the man in front of me was trying to sing along but he was crying too much. He was completely overcome. That was the point I turned my guitar right up and let it rip.

I drove back home straight after the show, as the next-door neighbour was getting married. I was still dancing, my heart fit to burst when the sun came up: so perfectly still, it was, and clement under the stars when I bounced out of the tent to cool down. The sound of music I never thought I'd hear again, then home to this, the commemoration of everlasting love. Love and music, the only enchantments we need. Joy and harmony everywhere, and I was drunk on it as I lay in the short grass, reflecting that people must have been doing silly dances in the moonlight around here for a long, long time, ever since they lived in the fort on the top of the next hill along. I could see one of the neighbours flinging herself around to 'Walking on Sunshine' in floods of unselfconscious delight, and other locals, arm-in-arm in a big circle kicking their legs and tossing their heads around. I wondered where Claire was and I didn't mind. She'll find me, I thought. How many stars was I looking at? I wondered. It was like trying to work out the number of leaves on a lime tree, impossible to guess. Easy to get it wrong by a factor of a thousand: many, many stars. And what strange tree did they all hang from? Nothing but music, I promise you. The sky gradually became simpler, just a lazy crescent of moon and the bright spot of Venus sitting side-by-side in the bottomless blue of forever. Immaculate England gently going green before my exhausted, exhilarated eyes. And there was my wife in the morning summer mist and she kissed me, touched my nose and said, 'Take me home.'

I'd been to see more or less everything Graham and Damon had done since Blur and I'd liked all of it. There is merit in everything both of them do. It was during the next show, an impromptu half a dozen songs at the Rough Trade shop, that I looked over at Damon and Graham and saw looks in both their faces that I hadn't seen since 1999. They were utterly in the music. We all were. We'd never played so well.

It was lovely wandering around with Graham again, going to St James to buy hats, the same things we had always done ten, twenty years ago, when we were at college even, but now there was no escaping ourselves. Our faces were plastered on walls as we wandered around town, on the front of newspapers, on flyposters reading 'Blur secret gig first reviews'. People recognised us and became hysterical. And then we left the world behind completely. We were on tour. At Southend, the first proper gig, the whole room went berserk. I've never seen a crowd behave like that, every single person in the house singing along, as one. Then back home to play Goldsmiths, where we'd met, so hot that it was raining on stage. All we could do afterwards was sit there in silence.

Claire was lent some jewellery to wear. It wasn't her thing – she didn't really like any of it – but there was a bracelet that I thought looked really good on the cat. I went to get everyone to show them how bling the old barnyard mouser was looking with his new necklace but he'd wandered off wearing it. Claire went rather pale. I thought they were crystals. They were diamonds, apparently. No one could find him but fortunately he did show up at feeding time as usual.

I stayed at the same hotel in Soho where I'd been staying for years but suddenly I found the staff were staring at me, that the manager was making a point of checking everything was OK. Then the owner called the room and made a point of checking everything was OK. It was all noise and eyes and movement. Briefly a Novotel in Wolverhampton, girls and shouting and sweating, then up to Newcastle and accustomising to the floating sensation of touring; gradually disconnecting from the routines of normal life and living in the moment from a suitcase. The tourbus pulled out of the huge shed of the MEN Arena in Manchester at midnight and steamrollered south through the night to Glastonbury, arriving about 4 a.m., after Phil Daniels had woken everyone up singing.

I didn't go to Glastonbury on Saturday. I went to see a cheesemaker just outside Shepton Mallet. I felt quite tense about the show and it was good to think about something else altogether, to try some experimental goat cheese.

Glastonbury was the big one. Glastonbury is an away gig really. It always sells out before the bill is announced so the crowd is not necessarily that friendly. A Glastonbury audience has very high expectations. There are a hundred things going on at any one time at Glastonbury and punters have to put themselves through insufferable indignities just to get to the Pyramid Stage. It was the ultimate test really. If we couldn't win over a neutral crowd, that was absolutely and definitely the end of Blur forever.

Backstage at Glastonbury is horrible. It is like a doctor's waiting room designed by Viking Office Supplies. The Gang Show at the Bournemouth Pavilion when I was in the Scouts had more pizzazz. Walking from the dressing room to the stage, which can take a while at big gigs, is where everything seems to start to happen in slow motion. My legs were actually shaking when we walked up the ramp. It was hard to see anything with the spotlights screaming in my face but it was still daylight when we started to play and I've never seen a crowd that big. It ran up the hill on either side of the stage, endless like an Escher painting. I reckon there were close on a quarter of a million people there. And they were waiting for something amazing to happen.

We started with 'She's So High'. The first song we wrote at our first rehearsal twenty-one years before and we nailed it. During 'Girls and Boys', the second song, we snapped the crowd, smashed it to bits. A mile away is about the distance that you see that someone has two legs. I couldn't tell how many legs the people on top of that hill had, but I could tell they were dancing and it just kept getting better. It was during 'Tender' that something changed forever. We finished playing the song, but the crowd wouldn't stop singing and even now as I write I'm shivering with goosebumps and grinning thinking about it. The Hyde Park shows were a slam dunk after that really. Even the weather was on our side. They were beyond any doubt the best gigs we've ever done. I have absolutely no idea if we'd ever play again, but if we didn't, that was a good place to leave it.

Back in the parish it was busy. Lines of cars in both directions and where the lines crossed, just outside fudgey, hoity-toity Stow-on-the-Wold, was a splat of almost unimaginable ugliness, stuck on the hillside. Civilisation slapped on top of nature like a Post-it note: the travellers' horse fair, caravans and trailers – horrible in the rain. At least as ugly as Glastonbury, it was, a locust mess of stinks, mud, stick men with too many teeth, blob women with none. Even as we arrived, before we'd parked the car, our hearts beat faster, a sense of danger, revellers shouting, impatience building with the traffic, the glamour of youth and glimmering thighs specked with mud.

What a scene inside that messy field! Another world altogether: a bonanza of lawlessness and frying. The things that catch the eye: dogs crammed in cages, tiny bulging ponies, spun sugar, plastic washing-up bowls with Dior and Chanel logos sprayed on. DVDs of bare-knuckle boxing bouts and then everything happening too fast, like an old film. I saw a man driving a trap and a man on horseback collide at high speed and it looked like it would come to blows. Most horrible of all was the man selling the fighting cocks: outsize, gnarly vulture-like things, all ready to rumble.

The blaring music, loud treacly cowboy-type songs, had completely brought me to a standstill shortly after we'd entered the field. 'Who's this playing now?' I said to the kid running the stall – all bootlegs laid out in front of him. 'Dunno,' he said, curling his lip and looking away. Quite comic, the sourness of his attitude against the schmaltzy sweetness of the music he was selling, but I couldn't blame him for that. I was an outsider and it's the travellers' day. They are not terribly popular with the locals and the mistrust is returned in equal measure. They always camped along the farm's borders in their wagons in high summer. I'd grown to rather like seeing them there.

People kept asking me whether I preferred cheese or music and I told them it was fine to have both, but it wasn't always possible. The Cheese Awards were held on the farm again but I missed them because the band were playing in Dublin. Claire saved me an exceptional piece of Cheddar. I was unable to resist. It kept me awake, luring me from my bed for a midnight nibble. Cheese tastes best in the middle of the night and I often made a journey to the fridge in darkness, but the Friday after the last show the whole house was bathed in moonlight.

Moonlight is a uniquely rural phenomenon. It's too subtle to compete with the background glow of the city. Even sunlight is at a premium in built-up areas, it's not really part of the package. Out here, sunshine dazzled through low windows as it rose and set and spent the rest of the day chasing everyone around.

There are probably only about thirty or so completely cloudless nights each year, and only one full moon a month, so a huge moon in a completely clear sky is a relatively rare occurrence. The moon was in a part of the sky where the sun never goes, casting odd shadows and suggesting that great things might be true. Everything looked new and beautiful in the pale silver radiance, like it might after a fresh fall of snow. It was definitely worth investigating so I stepped into the garden with my cheese, the grass cool, soft and moist under my feet. It was utterly still, not a breath of wind or a sound was stirring. The air was cool, but not cold, on my bare skin and the moonlight as subtle as the stillness of the air. It was a moment of perfect balance of the almighties of the Earth, Sun and Moon. I would go as far as saying it was, actually, magic. I went to get some more cheese.

The physical action of tilting my head back to look up at the night sky always gives me a pleasant tinge of vertigo. It's mildly exhilarating to look up any time of day, but at night I never know what it's going to start me thinking about, especially when I'm on my own. I always prefer it when it is an intimate situation, when I am alone with the rest of the universe. To be under the stars with someone you love is never a bad thing, but it's a different thing. The whole of the rest of the universe is easily eclipsed by the presence of a loved one, like moonlight in Leicester Square. Large groups of people are a non-starter for any kind of cosmic communion. They always scattered my thoughts. There is always someone who wants to know where the

Pole Star is and someone else who just wants to see a shooting star. Prolonged neck craning starts things aching, and pretty soon I always have to lie down. That's when I get really disorientated, or re-orientated. The earth's just a big funny magnet and we're all stuck on it. This is always more apparent to me when I'm lying on it looking down into space. Space is so near. If cars went up or down, or whichever direction space is in, they'd get there in under an hour. It's imminent, surely, I told myself as I nibbled a fresh piece of cheese.

High Noon. Fred had made his hay and the whole thirty-acre meadow was an immaculate lawn under a minimalist blue sky. It was all so simple and benign. *The New York Times* were back in the village, doing another feature about cheese, which they had declared was 'The New Rock and Roll'.

Things were knocking along as usual. The tilers finishing the roof of the new cheese lab had had a fight with each other and disappeared for a few weeks, but now they were back and happily banging away again. It was so hot in the afternoons that they'd been starting their banging at 5 a.m. and finishing before midday. There is always some kind of activity that involves banging occurring on a farm. Banging is a kind of heartbeat, and it didn't annoy me any more than the cock crowing.

The sense of buoyancy was still escalating, the entire neighbourhood was riding on the high tide of summer. I looked at the hamper I'd put together for a friend's birthday and wondered why they called this the simple life. It's not. It's complicated. The eggs, lamb and cheese that were in there represented a further education crammer course in everything I didn't know. I went down to the cellar to get some of Claire's Special Reserve pickle for the finishing touch, only to discover it had flooded again. The stream had backed up and there seemed to be a lot more frogs down there than usual. The beer barrel, the cider keg and bottles of wine and champagne were floating in two feet of spring water. Fortunately, the pickle was safe and presentable. I managed to wade through flotsam and jetsam and retrieve a jar and had soon located the source of the problem to a collapsed drain about half a mile from the house. I went to ask Fred if it was going to rain any more. He always knows these things.

'That drain collapsed twenty years ago,' he said. No, it wasn't going to rain 'til Tuesday at least. Five years before, if the cellar had flooded, I would have called the fire brigade. On Sunday, I thought, we'll sort this out tomorrow and went out to lunch.

You're unlikely to read much about drains in *The New York Times*, but this one was drawing a crowd of fascinated onlookers. It was news in the village. Blackham had heard about it before I had to tell him and was already down in the ditch – in what's known in the drain business as a 'gimp suit' – with a big smile on his face when I got there. Charlie the digger man had dropped in to have a look, too. Paddy called to say he'd heard about it.

The waters subsided as quickly as they came. By the evening the cellar looked like it had been cleaned rather than flooded.

While I'd been away the path down to the river had become overgrown again, the Sleeping Beauty, all nettles and jagged thorns. I fought my way through to the riverside where it was too hot to do anything except stare and I couldn't even stare very far or properly because it was hazy. It was like being underwater, a strange combination of light-headed weightlessness and friction. The cockerel had been all doodled out by noon. The sheep weren't taking much notice, as usual. It was still hard to say after all these years whether sheep were really cool or just really boring.

It was almost eerie. No emails, no phone calls, nobody and nothing, apparently. Just stifling stillness and clinging clothes. In the throttling grip of high summer it was left to things that buzz to suggest movement and keep me company.

I could just see the house back on top of the hill.

Houses are our monuments. I'd remarked to the builders some weeks back, when the steel trusses were being craned onto the stone walls of the new bit of the house, that building houses was, in quite a profound sense, really, sculpture. The steel guy said, 'That's not what we fackin' call it, mate.' The hay from the weekend harvest was assembled in a tower in the Dutch barn, like something the kids would build with extra-large Lego bricks, a precarious, primary work of art, built by Fred with a huge grin on his face.

A tableau, a picture, it was. There wasn't a single cloud in the sky and August sunshine was pouring out of the blue, pouring all over the valley, stoking a myriad shades of green to incandescence. Perhaps I was looking at the prettiest corner of the prettiest country in the world, at the prettiest time of year. There was nothing in that far-reaching view that wasn't beautiful to behold. Beyond giant wellingtonias and ancient cedars, the sheep, the steep impenetrable wooded valleys and a whiff of Wales some-where on the horizon. Captivating, it was. I caught an instantaneous, but cast iron glimpse of forever.

Something happens with boats, as they get bigger. The bigger and more expensive they get, the further away they take you from the thing they exist to present you with in the first place: the sea. Boats aren't really for going anywhere in. Boats are all about the sea and if you want to really feel the sea, it's best to sit in a tiny little boat. The biggest pleasure boats, no matter how fantastic – even the ones with a helicopter parked on one end and a submarine dangling from the other – are just like not very good hotels with small rooms that move around. It would be better to arrive at the desert island paradises, that all ocean-going gin palaces promise, in a tiny dinghy and camp ashore in a tent, rather than float around in a five-star bubble discon-nected from the world. It's easy to get swallowed by luxury. It can be a bigger obstacle to the world than poverty. This kind of thing happens with aeroplanes and caravans, as well. The bigger and more expensive they get, the further they remove their passengers from their element. And I'm beginning to wonder whether it's what happens to any person who becomes successful or important too, whether the isolation of the hero is implicit in any success story.

I've been to bigger houses, more expensive houses, but nowhere closer to paradise. I was home. What does success bring if not a quiet moment in the late afternoon sunshine? When getting home is more exciting than going away, that's all happily ever after can ever mean.

ACKNOWLEDGEMENTS

I've been writing about life on the farm for ten years now. Some of the things in this book may have appeared elsewhere, but it all really happened and all the people exist. And I'm still looking for the cricket pitch.

Buying a farm on our honeymoon was a completely ridiculous thing to do but it has been the making of me. I am forever grateful to everyone who has been a part of it.